Journey of Healing

Kathy Gruver, PhD

LOTUS PRESS

Box 325, Twin Lakes, WI 53181 USA
email: lotuspress@lotuspress.com
website: www.LotusPress.com

Previously Published by:
INFINITY PUBLISHING
Previously Published ISBN: 978-1-4958-0280-5

First Lotus Press edition 2017

ISBN: 978-0-9406-7647-3
Library of Congress Control Number: 2017958670

Printed in the United States of America

For information address:

LOTUS
PRESS
Lotus Press
Box 325, Twin Lakes, WI 53181 USA
email: lotuspress@ lotuspress.com
website: www.LotusPress.com

MORE AWARD-WINNING BOOKS FROM KATHY

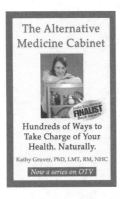

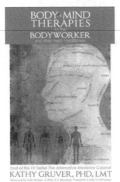

For a great general overview of natural health, please check out *The Alternative Medicine Cabinet*, which is a winner of the Beverly Hills Book Awards and now a TV series. If you are a practitioner, you will enjoy *Body/Mind Therapies for the Bodyworker* and *Market My Practice* for great and thorough business ideas. And *Conquer your Stress with Mind/Body Techniques* to learn everything you need to know about stress and how to stop your stress response. That book won **five awards** and I know you'll enjoy it! Please let me know how I can help.

www.theAlternativeMedicineCabinet.com

TABLE OF CONTENTS

Having fun during a photo shoot
Photo by Michael Cervin

Foreword by
Dr. Norman Shealy

As a Sagittarian, I have all too often rushed in and created an injury, from cuts and scrapes to broken bones and even ruptured discs. In 1971, I did one of my most stupid tricks – I tried to get on a green-broke gelding and wound up on the ground on the other side with a fractured hip. Six weeks later I was healed and back at my all-time favorite sport, racquetball. The Y where I played had a massage therapist and I had my first massage. It was glorious and I was hooked. I even hired the massage therapist to come work in my clinic and give all my patients massage. Forty-four years later, I remain devoted to massage.

I have had seventy-six Rolfing sessions, forty-four Alexander sessions, Bowen Work, Shiatsu, Schnelle Work and hundreds of variations. All massage is good; some is divine. I am convinced that just adding massage once a week, as I have, keeps my body far more supple and comfortable. Obviously there are many other essentials for optimal health—nutrition, exercise, daily habits and, above all, health consciousness. In fact I think CONSCIENTIOUS attention to all of health is by far the most important trait for health and longevity. And as *Journey of Healing* offers, many other health enhancers.

For twenty-six years, I have done a weekly radio call-in program on KWTO 560 in Springfield, Missouri. In that time I have probably recommended all of the many approaches discussed in this book. Massage is indeed great for everyone, but a more Holistic approach is essential. *I highly recommend that you read and follow the wise advice in this book in your personal healing journey.*

C. Norman Shealy, MD, PhD
Founder and CEO, National Institute of Holistic Medicine
Author of *Living Bliss*

DEDICATION

I always wanted to write an autobiography. I think I started my first one in seventh grade and then realized it would be more of a pamphlet than a novel. But I knew I'd get to tell my stories eventually.

As I was doing more radio and TV as a health and stress expert, people started asking me more about who I was and how I came to do what I do, rather than what I actually do. They had more personal questions; they wanted to know how in the world I starting doing flying trapeze or how a middle-aged white woman took such a passion and joy in hip-hop dance. What inspired me to help people with massage and what was it like to have a parent with cancer?

The fact that I have so many unusual and fascinating hobbies like spelunking, rappelling, ziplining, etc., was of real interest to people. They told me I was fascinating. They said that the things I did make them want to get off the couch and live their dreams too. Three words from my high school days echoed in my head: *Go for it*. I don't know where it came from or why I gravitated toward it at such a young age but it really seemed to be my mantra. I don't have a tattoo and I don't plan on getting one but if I did I honestly think I would have "Go for it" written in my father's handwriting on my forearm.

So here it is, my fifth book, the combination autobiography and textbook. Here you will find not only personal stories about my life and my journey but also the healing modalities that I've used to help heal myself and millions of others.

So many people have inspired me over the decades and I hope I can in that way be an inspiration to you. Enjoy.

I have lost several of my friends and clients in the last few years. So this book is written in their memory: Doug, Alice, Dorothy, Cathy, Dawn, Laurie. I've lost so many others and they are not forgotten.

This book is also written in my mother's memory. Without her going through her struggle and journey with cancer I would be a completely different person. I look back and feel so sorry at the suffering she endured. And I know she is in a way happier, better place.

This book is dedicated in a big part to my father, whose mantra also seems to be "Go for it." He was the first one to play football with us on the street and the first one to encourage me to try things out of my comfort zone. Though I still don't think he quite understands me, he's always been supportive. And though I'm not a parent, I am a child and can tell you he's the best parent ever, the perfect balance of saying yes and saying no.

To my clients and friends and people who would listen to my radio shows, who encouraged me to tell my story, laughed at my jokes whether or not they were funny and cheered as I did flying trapeze on the pier in Santa Monica. In fact, this is also dedicated to my trapeze friends: Christina, Blaine, Sean, Brian, Carl, Andrea, Brad, Richie and everyone at TSNY in Santa Monica and Emerald City in Seattle. To Tamarr Paul, the best damn dance instructor and choreographer EVER. And all the rest who encourage me to do my best.

Thanks to Hilary Hope for another phenomenal book cover and to Flo Selfman for her marvelous eagle eye editorial review.

And lastly, to my fabulous husband Michael. Without his love and support and constant encouragement and praise I would not have been able to accomplish half the things I did. I love you.

JOIN ME WON'T YOU ON THIS JOURNEY OF HEALING

Photo by Michael Cervin

FOR YOUR INFORMATION

A lot of the techniques I discuss in this book take much training and dedication to learn. Please seek out a qualified practitioner to work with when exploring these new modalities. And if your first experience with a certain method doesn't work for you, try someone else. Many practitioners have different ways of doing the same thing.

And I realize that not everything I talk about will resonate with every reader. I don't advocate any one modality or technique over another; I'm just giving you a buffet of health options along with my personal tales. Take what works for you. And please use a clean plate each time.

Also, a reminder that I am _NOT_ a medical doctor and this book is not meant to take the place of your healthcare provider. I am not intending to diagnose or treat any illness.

A quote from _The Teaching of Buddha_

II The Theory of Mind-Only

1. Both delusion and Enlightenment originate within the mind, and every existence or phenomenon arises from the functions of the mind, just as different things appear from the sleeves of a magician.

3. Therefore, all things are primarily controlled and ruled by the mind, and are created up by the mind.

One who is able to enjoy the purity of both body and mind walks the path to Buddhahood.

INTRODUCTION:
MY STORY

I've been involved in natural health and alternative medicine practically my entire life. When I was a kid I was drawn to massage and had a full imaginary medical practice for all my stuffed animals. I actually kept charts of their shots and when my mom would give me little Smarties candies to put in the pill containers, I would ration them out as if they were real medication, not just eat them like most kids would. I read my parents' college textbooks, the psychology and biology especially interesting to me. The clear plastic anatomy overlays were fascinating. But even though my faux veterinary practice thrived, I never had a desire to enter the field of medicine.

I was an Actress. An *Artiste*. I was going to entertain the masses and be the next big thing in Hollywood. I started performing in fifth grade and was hooked. I spent my entire life dancing, and acting came naturally as well.

My childhood took an unexpected dramatic turn when my mother was diagnosed with a rare cancer on her spine. My carefree only-child existence shifted to one of years of watching my mother suffer through chemo, radiation, multiple surgeries, losing her hair, addiction to morphine, constant vomiting and what I can only imagine was inconceivable pain. She lost her battle way too young, when she was not quite forty-six. I was newly eighteen.

Many people assume, understandably, that this experience with my mom was what propelled me forward into the healing arts. But I can say it wasn't. You can't come through an experience like that and have it NOT affect you, but I can't say A=B=C. What that childhood did was provide me with the urge to find options, not settle for the one solution presented, for anything. Because my mother wasn't given many options. Pittsburgh in the '80s didn't offer many alternatives for her. I remember asking about things like acupuncture and herbs, but the looks told all. Was I crazy? The one thing I do remember was my mom being given a hypnosis tape. One side was the ocean; the one thing that brought her great joy was our yearly vacations in Virginia Beach. The other side, I think, was a guided meditation for pain...or sleep. I think she listened to it once. What she did do was pray and, being Catholic, she put great faith in the Virgin Mary. Miraculous Medals were pinned to every housecoat and nightgown and statues lined the room. Clearly Mary desired her closer because the healing never came and the cure was missing. I remember being frustrated that no one had options for her. But as a kid, what did I have to offer? I remember reading books about psychic healing and charged water, gemstones and plants. But I had no power to intervene. My father was an angel to her, acting pretty much as nurse 24/7. If anything, he was a large inspiration to me, showing me compassion in care and patience, which I didn't always have as a teen.

But sorrowful stories aside, my life now is filled with helping others find healing, through my hands-on work, my books, my speeches and my media appearances. I couldn't help my mom, but in her memory, I can help countless other people find options for healing.

So, this book is just that. Options. Not everything will work for you. Not everything will make sense to you or fit into your belief structure, but with this buffet, take what you will and leave the rest for another. We are all on an individual journey and we cannot judge or imagine what another is here for, or what path they walk. I wish that you all find completeness and healing in your lives. And hopefully this book will act as a beacon of choice.

Go For It:
Living Life to Its Fullest

W hen I was in high school, my catchphrase was "go for it." For some reason, even though I had some social anxieties, I felt that things should just be gone for. I did not have a lot of friends in junior high and high school. I felt kids didn't like me, and I didn't relate well to them. So I was teased, bullied and picked on. I was beaten up one day after school, though I gave the girl a good run for her money until she put her hand over my nose and mouth and I couldn't breathe. I became very afraid of standing at the bus stop and going to school. Luckily that correlated with the time that I was given a parking permit to drive to school. Life became much easier for me.

When I discovered theatre my sophomore year of high school, everything turned around. I found a group of friends who accepted me and loved me for who I was. So many of those people are still my good friends today. But I digress. "Go for it." "Just do it," to quote Nike – the brand, not the goddess. You might find it strange that I'm talking about this in a health book. But I see so many people around me living in a place of fear. They are afraid to make a different choice, afraid to try new restaurants or even drive a different way to work, let alone question their doctor.

There is a certain comfort in our knowns. Even if our knowns are bad, we cherish them. The wife who will not leave the abusive husband. The man who will not leave a terrible job. The kid who goes to school for a major she has no interest in because that's what her parents want. When I tell people what I do and how I live, they say, "I wish I could do that." *You can.* Even if trapeze or massage or hiphop is not your thing, you can try something else. You don't have to be fully influenced by those around you.

During the time I was finishing up my PhD, I had a client in my office who remarked that it must be nice to be in school for something that you really want to do. I questioned as to whether she was also getting her PhD. She was, but didn't feel drawn to the psychology path that she was about to undertake. It was her parents' dream. I asked her what she would like to do. She said she'd like to be a baker. I asked, "Have you ever worked in a bakery?" She replied no. My assignment to her was to get a job or internship at a bakery that summer. I pointed out, how do you know if that's truly what you want to do if you never explore it? She laughed and agreed. I doubted that she would do it. When I saw her a few months later she was ecstatic to tell me that she had worked for a week in a bakery in town. I excitedly asked her if she liked it. She replied, "I hated every second of it. But now I feel more excited about psychology." Had she not done that, had she not taken that chance to explore another option, she would've wondered the rest of her life if she was on the right path. Go for it.

At what point must we make choices, make changes, and take risks? I value that I live my life this way. I take calculated risks. At least to me. You may disagree, as do a lot of people around me. I wanted to jump off cliffs and do flying trapeze, jump out of airplanes and take a risk with my business. I buy stocks that excite me even though they might go down in value, but it's all calculated. I don't play if I can't lose the money. I don't try it if I don't think I'll survive. As I'm writing this chapter, I just finished planning my trip to Jordan and Egypt. Many, many people are incredibly excited for me; many, many people think I'm crazy and they're afraid I'm not going to come home. At what point do you stop living because it's scary? It has been my dream since I was five to stand before the pyramids; I cannot turn down this opportunity. But it's calculated, I have done my research, I am taking my precautions and I am having private tours with an escort and driver. I'm not going to go driving into the desert in a Jeep, donning a bikini, singing *The Star-Spangled Banner*. There are ways to go for it and still be safe.

So the point of this chapter is saying, live life to its fullest. Explore your options, because we always have them. Know that with every exhale, you have the ability to make a different choice. A choice in your life, the way you love, and the way you live. Go for it. Three simple words can enhance your spiritual, mental and physical health. Why sit idly by when the world is so big around us. Your assignment is to do something different tomorrow. Drive a different way to work, sit in a different desk in class, start your meal with dessert first, try a new restaurant, get out of the wrong side of the bed and take a shower using only your left hand. Stretch yourself. Stretch your imagination and your boundaries and you will find that so much abundance comes to you. They say God helps those who help themselves. You can't help yourself sitting in fear. Go for it. Live large, laugh aloud and love deeply.

Massage and Bodywork: Rub Me the Right Way

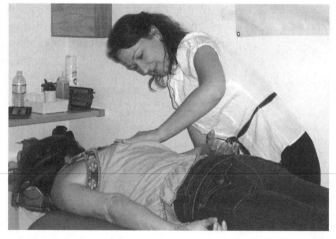

Kathy doing massage at an event

E very journey has a first step. Mine was very accidentally massage. I have a clear memory of being five or six, sitting behind my dad in the car on one trip to Virginia and massaging his neck so he didn't get a headache. And that apparently was the start of my healthcare career. I would sit in the chorus room in high school and people would plop down in front of me and request a shoulder rub. Apparently I had a skill that I wasn't even aware of. Or we were just happy to have someone of the opposite sex touch us.

When I got into college I was a theatre major. My life was going to be performing, on the stage, on the screen, on the TV; anywhere anybody would pay me (or sometimes not) to perform. However, once again my life took an unexpected turn the summer between my freshman and sophomore years when I helped out on the crew for our children's theatre performance of *Treasure Island*. Since the cast was all men, I got to be on crew. My big responsibility for the show was changing the pirate flag at intermission.

Our first week of rehearsal was certainly a very exciting time and everyone got even more excited as a short older woman walked through our hallway carrying bags of who knew what. Everyone rushed down the hall and I asked what was happening. Somebody said, "Dr. Pat is here." I had to see for myself. I followed the throngs of people down the hallway to find this woman unpacking bags of mats and teas and herbs. An assistant behind her like a Sherpa carried a large container for tea. Someone immediately started a list and people clamored to sign up. I had to know what this woman was doing. I sat down and watched as she did massage and bodywork on the actors – for free, I might add. This had been the third or fourth year that she joined us for the summer, I learned. She would work on us for free, knowing that we were working so hard to do two shows a day, five days a week, for six weeks during the summer. It was an award-winning children's theatre. We weren't just putting on cute outfits and prancing around pretending we were adults. We were doing full-scale productions. For example, *Treasure Island*, the show that I was in, had a full-scale pirate ship on the stage with battles and melees and swordfights and people swinging from a rope. Long John Silver had a peg leg and a real bird that sat on his shoulder – Capt. Flint; what a great little creature.

So the times that she was there that summer I would sit and I would watch and I would learn and finally near the end of that summer she turned to me exhausted and said, "Kathy I've got to get to my other job. Can you take those mats and go in the other room and work on Bill?" I looked at her like she was crazy and said, "I don't know what I'm doing." She looked very deeply into my eyes and the music swelled and she said, "Yes, you do." I stared back and at that moment I had the sense to listen to her. I took the mats and I worked on the other student and I was really, *really* good at it. She saw something in me that I didn't know existed. And it was one of those times where another's influence helped me understand myself better.

For three summers I worked with her whenever I could. When I wasn't on stage and when she was there, you could be sure I was sitting in the corner handing her herbs and creams, watching what she was doing and soaking in all the information. Right before I was done with school and about to move to California, I realized I really did have a gift for massage and I asked her where I could go to study and get certified. She laughed and said, "Geez, I'll certify you." It was a different time then. I went home that weekend and told my dad I was considering something like chiropractic school. He laughed and said, "Like hell you are." He had just put me through four years of school. But I did decide that when I landed in Los Angeles I would formally study massage. And I did.

What a change that was. Having never worked on a massage table before, I had done everything on the ground and I didn't know the terms, the muscles or anything. When the gentleman at the massage table store asked me if I'd been doing shiatsu all these years, I had no idea what he was talking about. I figured I better at least pretend I knew what I was talking about so, in addition to the table, I looked across the room and said very confidently, "Oh, you should give me one of those boisters too." He looked confused. It was a bolster. I had misread it.

So I can credit the lovely woman all those years ago during *Treasure Island* as starting my health career. I tip my hat to her, as I owe her quite a bit. And that was about twenty-five years ago. I studied in Los Angeles and Santa Barbara and a school out of Florida, and with every single client, I learn more and more. Following are some of the benefits of massage and also some of the different types of massage that you can get in your local spa and health center and also some information about becoming a massage therapist yourself.

Massage in Egypt?

Massage has been around for centuries; in fact, it is believed that evidence of massage was discovered in hieroglyphics in ancient Egypt. We know massage feels good, but what else does it do for us?

Research has shown that massage lowers blood pressure and heart rate, can lower and stabilize blood sugar, help preterm infants with growth, decrease stress and increase feel-good hormones like oxytocin. It also moves lymph throughout your body. What is lymph? Lymph is the cleansing system of the body. It runs through vessels similar to your circulatory system, but doesn't have a pump (like the heart) to move it. So lymph is moved through your body from movement, breathing, muscle contraction and massage. The more the lymph moves through, the better your immune system, as the lymph carries away the "bad stuff." In a situation involving cancer, however, you don't want those cells moving through the body via the lymph. If you've had cancer, please tell your practitioner up front.

Massage helps with circulation, which is why it is so good for elderly people or those who are inactive due to injury or sedentary work. Massage helps move the blood and fluid around, which is extraordinarily beneficial in healing. People with swollen legs and ankles, like pregnant women or those with lymphedema, can find relief with massage.

Just being touched is another benefit for the elderly. It is relaxing, nurturing and can improve their quality of life. It's also shown to have a huge benefit for kids, as there often is so little healthy touch for them.

When we think of massage we think of muscles and that is the main part of the body that massage addresses. After a workout, our muscles produce toxins like lactic acid. We want to move those out of the body to avoid muscle tiredness or pain. Massage flushes those toxins, smoothes the muscle fibers and helps relax them. Massage techniques like **deep tissue** and **trigger point massage** actually help stretch out the muscles. Massage helps with muscle injuries by bringing healing blood to the area, but make sure you are not having deep tissue done on a muscle tear; that can cause more problems! I've seen massage help with headaches, low back pain, knee pain, even abdominal pain. Seek out a qualified practitioner.

A technique called **myofascial release** can help those muscles even more by loosening up the fascia. What is fascia, you ask? When you take the skin off a raw chicken breast, there is a shiny film that lies over the meat; that is the fascia. It is between the muscle and skin and helps support our movements. Sometimes the fascia gets bound to muscle and restricts our range of motion. Myofascial release works on unbinding that fascia to allow us less-restricted movement and freedom.

Whereas massage used to be seen as just a luxury, more and more research is being done on its health effects. Some of the current research is showing that massage reduces nausea in cancer patients, decreases pain after surgery, reduces hospital stays, reduces anxiety and depression and helps colicky infants relax and sleep better.

Massage loosens tight muscles by stretching out muscle fibers, bringing blood to the area, flushing out toxins and eliminating trigger points. Trigger points are tight bands of muscle that refer pain in a specific pattern. For example, you may have a trigger point under your shoulder blade that is actually referring pain up into your neck. Eliminate the point, eliminate the pain. Massage is also great for improving circulation and reducing swelling in the limbs (great for the elderly). **Lymph drainage massage** is a specific modality that works by flushing the lymph out of the limbs, back to the lymph nodes found in the armpits, groin and neck. There are times you don't want to move lymph, however, and, again, that is when cancer is involved. There is a chance of spreading it further through the body. Check with your oncologist to see if massage would be safe for you.

Massage can improve flexibility and help with athletic performance. Massage is also a great post-exercise addition as it gets the toxins out that may have built up during the sport. It can also help with muscle cramping and helps reduce scar tissue, thus freeing up movement.

Massage calms and invokes what is known as the Relaxation Response. This is in opposition to the stress response, that fight-or-flight reaction. Massage releases feel-good hormones in the brain like oxytocin. Oxytocin is what mothers produce during labor. It makes us feel good and kind and loving toward others. And massage calms the entire system. Massage has been shown to lower blood pressure and slow heart and respiratory rates. We are seeing more and more research being done on the benefits of a good rubdown. The findings include reduced depression and anxiety, better heart health, improved health for preterm infants and better sleep.

Though massage is proving to be a valuable addition to your life, there are a few things that it doesn't do. Massage is not going to help you lose weight or reduce cellulite. It could act as a temporary fix by flushing the toxins out of the area, but ultimately the cellulite will return. Sorry. Also, massage does not give you the flu. I've had a few clients tell me they don't want deep tissue because they don't want to get sick. I can't say they didn't have the flu. I can say that the massage didn't give it to them. What they were experiencing was a healing crisis or Herxheimer reaction. This occurs when toxins are mobilized too fast and they settle back in the body rather than being eliminated. Though uncomfortable, a healing crisis is perfectly normal and can be avoided by drinking lots of water after your massage, stretching, taking it easy and, for some people, taking a pain reliever like Advil.

Here are some tips for better enjoyment of your massage.

When you go for your massage, communicate openly with the therapist about what your expectations are and if you have any injuries, illnesses or recent surgeries that they should be aware of. If you are uncomfortable during the massage, especially if something is hurting, please tell the therapist. You must communicate this to them for your own safety and enjoyment.

Most therapists will have you fully disrobe; however, there are some modalities that don't require that, like shiatsu, Thai massage and Reiki. Check with the practitioner for guidance.

For general relaxation, choose a modality like **Swedish**, which is the basic, light-touch massage. Deep tissue and trigger point are better for pain, increasing range of motion, for athletes and people who want more intense work done. Be careful of hot stone massage. If you are going to have that done, make sure the person is well trained, as an inexperienced therapist can hurt you.

Find a qualified practitioner for what you need. Regulations for licensing vary from state to state, sometimes city to city. Ask how long they've been practicing and be picky. Be careful of some of the new shopping center massage chains, as often their therapists are fresh out of school and not very experienced. This might be fine for a general relaxing massage, but if you have an injury or health concern, they might not have the experience to help you.

Here are some tips on how to communicate with your massage therapist and other health practitioners.

Communication is defined as *the science or practice of transmitting information.*[1] But just as important as transmitting information is receiving and processing it. When working with people such as a massage therapist or natural health professional, clear communication, both verbal and nonverbal, is key to getting the experience you are seeking.

Communication doesn't start when you get on the table. Before you even meet the therapist, you have an opportunity to implement clear communication skills.

Check on price and the amount of time you get for that price. It might be advantageous to see if you have the option of going longer at the time of the massage. And are you really getting an hour, or is it a 50-minute-hour situation?

---

[1] The Oxford Essential Dictionary. 1998 Oxford University Press, pg. 114.

Find out the cancellation and no-show policy and adhere to it if you must cancel. Many spas will take a credit card to hold your appointment and will charge you if you don't show. Please respect their time.

Tell the therapist why you are coming to see them and the results that you expect. This can save you disappointment, time and money, as they might not even specialize in what you are looking for.

Once the appointment has been made, make sure you have their address and correct directions/parking instructions. Ask for their cell phone number and get specific instructions to their office if you need them. And please be respectful and write it down; don't assume you will remember. If they are coming to you, give them your address and any unusual parking information like street cleaning on certain days, etc., or if there are a lot of stairs. Those tables get really heavy and awkward up a large staircase.

Once you meet the therapist, clear communication of your expectations and needs is crucial.

Most therapists want to know how you found them and appreciate it if you volunteer that information.

Fill out the intake form completely and bring to their attention anything particularly unusual or that needs explanation.

Mention any illnesses, injuries, previous surgeries, bumps, bruises, cuts or herpes outbreaks. (This last item might be embarrassing, but is important nonetheless, as the therapist is vulnerable to contracting it by touching any sores.)

Tell them how you like your pressure, if there is anything that needs to be avoided or if you would like them to focus on a particular area or issue.

If you are a first-timer, you'll want to find out how this therapist works. For example, do you disrobe completely or do they prefer underwear to be left on? It's okay to be nervous your first time and to even share this feeling with the therapist. Your therapist can typically sense your discomfort, and will do their best to make you feel relaxed and comfortable.

If you're not familiar with massage, have them explain some of the benefits and tell them specifically what you expect. For example, "I have really bad headaches. I'm looking for some relief." Or "I really just want to relax and unwind."

If the therapist asks you, "How are you feeling?" be as specific as possible with your answers so the therapist can address what ails you. Answers like "Fine" or "I feel bad" do little to enlighten the therapist to your specific needs.

If you have had massage before, it's perfectly acceptable to tell the new therapist what you liked and didn't like about the last therapist. I have had therapists shove their oily fingers in my ears. I don't like that. Who would? I tell every new therapist *not* to do that to me.

And if you like to have your massage in silence, saying that up front is a good idea. Don't assume the therapist will pick up on it once the massage has started. However, if they chatter on through the entire massage and don't get the hints that you want silence, you might want to find a new therapist.

Make it clear if you need to have anything adjusted once the massage has begun, such as the temperature, the music and the pressure. They should change whatever is not working for you. It's your time and the treatment should be personalized for you.

Many spas automatically use hot towels. If this is something you prefer to not have, ask if this is part of their treatment and tell the therapist you would like to skip it.

Tell the therapist if you'd like a whole body massage or if you just want certain areas concentrated upon. Sometimes if you mention certain tension spots, the practitioner may get carried away and run out of time for the rest of your body. You might be okay with that or want work elsewhere. Clarify so they know.

After the massage:

Ask questions if you have them.

It is important to drink water and do light stretching.

Reschedule another appointment. Some therapists like myself get very booked and you may have to wait several weeks for an appointment if you don't rebook immediately.

Remember that permanent changes rarely occur with the first session, so you may need more work.

If you have had deep work, you may be sore and ice might be appropriate.

If you want to become a regular client, ask if you can have a standing appointment or if there is a price break for buying more than one. Many therapists will give you discounts for purchasing a series, such as 10% off or buy five, get the sixth free.

In order to receive the most benefit from massage, you need to feel comfortable and relaxed. A big part of this is developing a sense of trust and understanding between you and your therapist. In such a personal relationship as massage, we can see how interpersonal communication can make or break this experience. Be open and concise, truly listen, choose your words carefully and remember that more information is better than none.

What follows now is a basic description of the most common massage techniques.

Swedish is the most basic massage technique. It addresses the outer layer of muscle, therefore doesn't go as deep or effect as much change on the body as other techniques. Also considered classic massage, this is what you are going to get in most spas. It tends to be the least expensive on the menu and also in my opinion the least effective. Used for general relaxation, feel-good massage.

Deep tissue tends to be an upcharge in spas and it addresses the deeper layers of muscle. Contrary to popular belief, it doesn't have to hurt. Deep tissue is not just harder Swedish and takes extra training. If you want this modality, make sure the practitioner knows what he/she is doing. You can get hurt with an inexperienced practitioner. Good for injuries and rehab if the therapist is experienced.

Sports massage incorporates a lot of deep tissue techniques and is used for pre- and post-event therapy. Also often involves shaking of the limbs, stretching and flushing. Used mostly for athletes.

Hot stone is a popular spa treatment. Though few massage therapists do it, it accounts for the most injuries and massage lawsuits. I'm not a fan of this modality, as you can get burned or an inexperienced therapist can't feel the tissue beneath the stone and goes too deep. Personally, I find this pointless. (Just my opinion.) There is usually an upsell charge. Pregnant women should not have this done.

Reiki is not a massage technique; it's energy work. It's often incorporated into massage practices and typically costs more. A session is between 60 and 90 minutes and involves hands-on healing, which helps a person heal on all levels of body, mind and spirit. Many hospitals and cancer centers use this technique. It's great for emotional issues as well as on people who can't have regular massage, such as cancer patients. Good for anyone with physical issues or emotional/spiritual stress. See full chapter on Reiki on page 25.

Shiatsu is Japanese massage, which is done fully clothed on mats on the floor. This is why the clerk in the massage store asked if this was the technique I've been doing since I told him I had never worked on a table. Shiatsu involves acupressure points and compression and is great for balancing the body. It is used more for balancing chi and less for physical ailments. Not done much anymore that I've seen. Some spas have adapted it for a table, which confuses people because then they go to an actual shiatsu practitioner and are stunned that they stay dressed and on the floor.

In general, massage is not covered by insurance. Because we are not licensed practitioners like doctors or chiropractors, there is no continuity of care between states or individual practitioners. I can bill Workers' Comp and personal injury with an Rx because I do medical massage. Often car accident insurance will pay for massage, but Workers' Compensation is getting pickier.

I have truly loved my time as a massage therapist and even though I have grown my practice into other modalities and focuses, I still value every client and every moment of massage. If this is a path you think you'd like to pursue, here are a few tips. Or feel free to skip this section and read on.

You've graduated from massage school; you have your table, sheets, lotion and ridiculously short nails. Now what? This is a question we all asked ourselves as we stepped out into the real massage world. There are numerous options for you. Here are just a few. Depending on your personality, skill set and how much you want to work, any of these options might work for you. You might want to start your own practice, join someone else's, work for a spa or massage company or join up with a chiropractor, physical therapist or other complementary practitioner.

No matter where you end up working, here are some must-haves. If you want more in-depth info about starting and building a massage practice, please pick up a copy of my book *Market My Practice*, available on my site www.thealternativemedicinecabinet.com.

–Business cards. Even if you're working in a spa or for someone else, people should have a way to contact you. It can simply be your name and contact number, but make sure it looks professional. I recommend www.vistaprint.com where you can get free or very inexpensive business cards. Don't get too cute or complicated; simple is best. And once you have the cards, don't be caught without them. I've gotten clients in line at supermarkets, at parties and in parking lots because I had a business card on hand. You can also post them on bulletin boards around town; you never know when you might need one. I got a great speaking gig from a gal I met at a Van Halen concert – because I had a card.

–A dedicated phone line. It's best if you can avoid using your home phone as your business line. There are numerous reasons. The first is your own safety. If someone shady starts to get out of hand, they won't have your home phone number, which means they won't have your home address and can't show up at your door. Aside from safety, you'll know your roommate, spouse or small child isn't going to miss calls, not give you messages or accidentally be rude to a potential client.

When you answer the phone, do so professionally, saying your name. Make sure your outgoing voice message is concise and professional. Don't make people wait through five minutes of *Stairway to Heaven*; just say your name, business name and any other pertinent information. Check messages regularly and return calls promptly. I've gotten numerous clients because I'm the only therapist who actually called them back.

–I know this sounds stupid, but have a massage table. And enough sheets and oil. I had someone apply for an outcall therapist position that I was trying to fill and halfway through the phone call they informed that they didn't have a car…or a table. I'm still wondering how they thought they were going to be an outcall massage therapist.

–You may want to invest in a laundry service, which both provides you with your sheets and then launders them, or at the very least using a Laundromat, which will wash and fold them for you. I had just started my business and I was doing all my own laundry. I got a call one day for a massage and had to turn it down because I had no clean sheets. What business was I in? Laundry or massage? The next day I found the laundry service that I still use to this day.

–Make sure you get insurance. Many of the insurance companies give you a special deal while you're still in school so you can take advantage of that. Two of the biggies are ABMP (www.abmp.com) and AMTA (www. amtamassage.org). Being a member of one of these organizations provides not only insurance, but also listings on massage search engines, information about licensing requirements in your area, continuing education opportunities, a magazine subscription and a level of professionalism. And most spas and employers will want to see a proof of insurance.

Now that we've covered some of the basics, here are some employment options for you. Even if you're not a massage therapist, you might find these pros and cons interesting. After you graduate from massage school, you're ready to step out into the world of employment. Some students know from the get-go what their objective is and others struggle to find their place in the massage world. Here are a few options to explore as you expand your massage resume and find your niche. Before trying to narrow down your job options, my advice is to look back through your training and see what modalities you enjoyed most. If you liked Swedish and hot stone, then a spa is more likely to thrill you than a physical therapy office. On the other hand, if anatomy was your best subject and you loved learning about trigger point therapy, then perhaps a PT office or chiropractic clinic might be more appropriate for you.

Here is a breakdown of the most common massage employers.

Spas

When you think of massage, a spa definitely comes to mind. Whether it's a private spa or one contained in a hotel or resort, the structure is pretty much the same. Most will require insurance, licensing and an interview/hands-on demonstration. The payment structure of spas can vary from being on-call (showing up only when needed) or having set hours where you wait at the facility for someone to need you. When quoted what you will be paid, clarify what they are paying you for.

Most spas only pay for hands-on time, and the time you sit and wait will either be unpaid or at a drastically reduced rate, like minimum wage. Also, some establishments will expect you to do other duties when not massaging, like folding towels, cleaning and stocking supplies.

Clarify during the interview the payment structure and what is expected of you. If it's a situation where multiple therapists are waiting for work, you might want to find out about how they pick the therapist for the client. Is it seniority? Determined by shift time? Skill level? The last thing you want is to sit around a room, making minimum wage, and not ever getting your hands on someone.

Downside:

Spas tend to be pricey, but the percentage that goes to the therapist can be low.

You might be sitting around for work where you often don't get paid for your time.

Possibly a demanding clientele (of course, that can happen anywhere).

Strict rules such as no talking to the client or having to follow a very structured massage routine.

Upside:

The room, table, lotion, etc., are provided.

Good tips and steady work possible.

Medical Practice

The other end of the spectrum is a physical therapy or chiropractor's office. You need to have a good grasp of skills to work in this environment, knowledge of basic medical terms/SOAP notes, etc. and want to help people through their ailment or disability. Some offices will hire you full time and your tasks may involve note taking, prepping a patient with hot packs, e-stim, ultrasound, etc., or you may be called in to treat specific patients.

This type of work requires a certain personality, as sometimes you are dealing with people in a great deal of pain. It's also important that you take direction well, as oftentimes you'll be working directly under a doctor or therapist. This work can be extraordinarily rewarding and you may get to work with different populations such as athletes, the elderly or children.

Downside:

Pay is normally pretty low.

Dealing with people in pain can be trying.

Paperwork such as insurance forms and note-taking.

Upside:

Satisfaction of helping people recover.

Increased knowledge of the body and medical issues.

Massage Franchise/Chain

The newest outlets for massage are the national chain or shopping mall massage businesses. These are popping up all over the country and, though they are being met with mixed feelings, they are here to stay. Typically they encourage clients to sign up for packages that require a membership fee like a gym and then a certain number of monthly massages are included. This can be steady work and keep you busy but there are downsides as well. I have to admit I'm not a fan of this business model, as I see a lot of therapists being taken advantage of and treated horribly. The other problem for the public is many times these are new therapists who are not very well trained, so the client gets a horrible or dangerous treatment. I feel like one of these chains in particular has ruined the business of massage.

Often there is a big pressure to sell and if you don't meet a preset quota, you're met with some harsh words. Often the clientele are less than stellar, since this is a bargain environment. It's a good way to get experience because you do get better with everyone you touch. They may require you to sign a contract stating that you won't work for any other spa or facility within a certain radius. Think carefully about that. Is this going to provide you with enough work that you don't have to be on call elsewhere as well?

Downside:

A bargain environment can sometimes attract less-than-desirable clients.

Long hours/multiple clients back to back with no break, which is physically challenging.

Low wages.

Pressure to sell.

Non-compete clause.

Upside:

Steady work.

Great experience with multiple clients.

Self-Employment

Most people starting massage school have an idea that they will have a practice where they set their hours and rate and work for themselves. This is certainly an option once you graduate, but understand what that involves. There are many decisions to be made. Do you want to do outcall only or get an office? One is physically challenging and the other requires upfront and monthly costs. You must advertise your practice, pay for your own sheets, lotion, music, etc., bill clients, deal with scheduling, answer the phone, return calls, send reminders and follow-ups and, on top of all that, massage people. For detailed information about running your own business, see my book *Market my Practice* on my website.

It's an overwhelming task and not everyone is cut out for it. And that's okay. The rewards are great, you do get to set your own hours and price, but there is a cost for being your own boss. There is a lot of work involved and I think most people dive into it without really thinking it through. I remember rushing for the phone on weekends and evenings to make sure I didn't miss any calls, taking every massage that came in so I could build my client list. It was exhausting and time-consuming. If you are committed, driven, responsible and organized, it might be for you. Warning: it's not for the lazy or faint of heart.

Downside:

Time-consuming.

Wearing multiple hats.

Expense involved.

Huge commitment.

Must be constantly available and promoting yourself to succeed.

Upside:

Feeling of accomplishment.

Structure your practice to your dreams.

Select your hours, clients and rates (not right away, but once you become more established).

It's easier to find a niche and specialize if you are running your own practice.

Corporate Clients

Another new option that is becoming available in many parts of the country is corporate massage. You'd take your massage chair to offices or hospitals and perform short massages on staff or clients. This is fast-paced and fun and some companies allow you to hand out your own cards for anyone who wants a longer, private massage. Always check first before doing something like this, as not everyone allows it. Some allow you to accept tips, others don't, and again it's a great way to get your hands on many bodies to gain experience and confidence.

Chair massage at a corporate health event

Downside:

Lugging equipment.

Chair massage is physically difficult and can be tedious after several hours.

Upside:

Steady.

Diversity of environments and people.

Possibly leads to private clients.

Gym or Fitness Center

The last mention of employment options is the local gym. More and more are offering massage to their members. It's usually by appointment only and you'll be expected to have a grasp of sports massage and be prepared to work on athletes. This is great experience to get into the sports world and work on people who are conscious of their bodies. You can typically set your hours or it can be an on-call basis. The pay is pretty good and a lot of people tip.

Downside:

Confined to a gym setting.

By appointment only; might not be steady work.

Upside:

Built-in clientele.

Experience with athletes and body-conscious people.

These choices that I've mentioned here are by no means what you are limited to. Create your own options in salons, hospitals and airports. Massage is growing quickly in this country and the options will soon be limitless. Explore, knowing that you can always change your mind and make a different choice.

REIKI: THE NEXT STEP IN MY JOURNEY

As journeys go, sometimes we think we have a certain destination but something distracts us. Maybe it's a flat tire, maybe it's a beautiful sunset, but something takes us off course just for a moment. That's what Reiki was for me. It didn't divert me off course completely, but it added something of value to the trip. I had never heard of Reiki until, back in 1993, a close friend said, "Hey, you do massage and I just heard of this thing that you might really like." And I thought, "Ok," but didn't do a thing about it. And then the universe kicked in and made me pay attention. I saw an article on Reiki in a magazine I was reading. I saw books for it pop up in stores I was at. Someone asked me if I ever heard of it and on and on, as these things are wont to do. So, I paid attention. I bought a book on Reiki by Diane Stein called *Essential Reiki*. I read it cover to cover in practically one sitting and decided it was absolutely something I needed to do. It was about transmitting universal love energy through you and out of your hands to help speed the healing for others. But someone had to "attune" you. Where could I find that? I turned to a popular resource for this sort of thing in LA, the *Whole Life Times*. There were four ads for people doing Reiki. One ad turned me off completely. The other three were possible. One never called me back and the other I didn't jibe with on the phone. The fourth call was to a woman named Diane. My mind mixed up names and letters and I thought it was the same person who wrote the book that had propelled me onto the Reiki part of my journey. I connected with her immediately on the phone and made an appointment for my first Reiki I attunement.

She gave me handouts for the first level, taught me what Reiki was, the history, etc. And then gave me my first Reiki healing session. I lay on a massage table and she put her hands on various parts of my body starting with my head. She used a pendulum to check my chakras and used gemstones and crystals on those points that she deemed needed help. I felt heat from her hands and could see colors behind my eyes as she moved her hands to various spots. I was clothed and covered in a light blanket. After the session, which lasted about an hour, she did my attunement. I sat in a chair with my hands in prayer position in front of my heart. She alternated between standing in front and behind, did things to my hands and the top of my head. In just a few moments it was over. She gave me a banana (which was the best-tasting banana ever), told me to practice as much as I could and sent me on my way. And I did just that. I practiced on myself, my husband, friends, cats, a giant teddy bear, the fish...anything I could get my hands on (no pun intended). And I felt the energy growing.

I went back for a second attunement to strengthen it and it followed the same procedure. But then something changed. I wasn't at a great place in my life. I wasn't respecting myself or those around me. I went to a party, drank too much, misbehaved and I found the next time I went to do Reiki, it wasn't there. I couldn't bring the energy back to my hands. How was that possible?

I showed up at Diane's. I was embarrassed and stunned that this lovely energy could disappear as quickly as I had mastered it. So I had another attunement and it was even more amazing than the first. But, as youth are apt to do, I had another night of debauchery, this one even more extreme, and when I tried Reiki a few days later, it had once again left me. I was furious with myself. Not only was I wasting a huge amount of money, but I was clearly doing something to myself so that the energy couldn't be there any more. It was a true disappointment in myself. I had a deep heart-to-heart with Diane. She explained that Reiki was a gift of spirit and that if I wanted to be harmful and disrespectful to myself, then I wasn't worthy to have the gift. Was I worthy now? Yes, I was! So...I had my fourth Reiki I attunement. And it stuck. I made different decisions in my life. I decided that over-indulging in negative things clearly wasn't serving me. And I could still enjoy the parties, without the excess. This attunement lasted.

I moved quickly through the levels and after my second Level II attunement, Diane expressed that, should I like to move on to Master level, I was ready to do so. And I was ready; so I undertook the studying, learned how to pass attunements to others and did the Master level attunement. It was beautiful. She warned me in advance that this would change my life, that with this knowledge and energy, things couldn't stay the same. And they didn't. A few months after the attunement, I left my relationship, met a new man, and soon after moved to Santa Barbara, Calif., where I am now.

I still use Reiki in my practice, both as a stand-alone treatment and incorporated into massage. Reiki is fabulous to heal on all levels of body, mind and spirit. Many hospitals and cancer centers around the country use Reiki in their facilities. I've used Reiki on cancer patients, end-of-life situations, during labor and birth, for loss (one woman had just lost her baby) and to speed up wound healing. I have used Reiki on myself for all my surgeries and injuries (see chapter on surgery pg. 115) with great results. I sustained a small knife wound in the palm of my hand, scary for a massage therapist. I did Reiki on the wound while sitting in the ER and by the time the doctor saw me, the wound had healed so much he basically had to reopen it to clean it and put stitches in. At any rate, Reiki is phenomenal and really works. Here is some info about the history of this fabulous modality and how to find a practitioner.

Reiki is a hands-on healing energy technique where universal energy, or chi, comes through the practitioner and into the person being healed. It heals on all levels of body, mind and spirit. It is relaxing, balancing and strengthening.

I had my first Reiki attunement in 1994 from a teacher in Los Angeles. An attunement is basically another name for the initiation/procedure to give the healer the ability to use Reiki. An attunement consists of symbols placed in the hands and head of the soon-to-be healer. The attunement itself is a quick process, taking only a few minutes, but most Reiki teachers spend several hours if not days with the practitioner before the actual attunement.

There are three levels of Reiki: I, II and III (Master level). The first level gives you the ability to practice on yourself and others. The second provides you with symbols to enhance the practice and also work from a distance, and the third attunement teaches you how to teach others. That is called the Master level and, unlike the name implies, does *not* make someone at that level superior to others at the lower stages. It simply means that they can pass attunements and teach others.

Reiki, meaning Universal Light Energy, is thought to be as ancient as mankind itself and its roots are steeped in myth. It is based on a master/teacher relationship and on initiations of the students.

Reiki was re-discovered by a man who was looking for answers. Mikao Usui, a Christian minister and university professor, wanted to know how Jesus did his healing. A ten-year quest abroad and a seven-year search in the United States proved useless; no information could be found. Usui decided to embark on a journey.

He returned to Japan where he studied ancient texts in a Zen monastery but knew he needed to go through the "test." The test was a three-week fast and meditation. On the final morning of his quest, slightly before sunrise, Usui saw a bolt of light coming from the sky directly toward him. He felt fear and wanted to run, but realized this is what he had been waiting for. The light struck his forehead over his third eye and Usui lost consciousness. He saw millions of colorful bubbles and the Reiki symbols appeared to him along with information about how to use them. It was the first Reiki attunement.

Usui took Reiki through the streets of Japan and spent the next several years traveling, healing and sharing his story. It was believed that Usui made 16-18 Reiki Masters in his career, but only one was mentioned in most Reiki sources and was Usui's successor, Dr. Chujiro Hayashi. This man went on to teach Reiki, open a healing clinic and made sixteen Masters in his lifetime.

Though information on Reiki, once kept secret, is available in every bookstore and on countless websites, even eBay, it's a unique skill in that you must have someone teach you. You can read all the books you want, but without the hands-on attunement, it just won't work. I do believe that some people are born with Reiki ability, but most experts concur that having a teacher, a guide, is necessary. It helps you to hone your skill and provides you with more focus and intention.

How Reiki works is pretty simple. You place your hands on the person (or above the body) with the intention of healing, and the energy starts to flow. It often feels like a heat and tingling in the hands. There is usually a deep sense of relaxation for the person enjoying the session and they may even fall asleep. Sometimes laughter or tears come too.

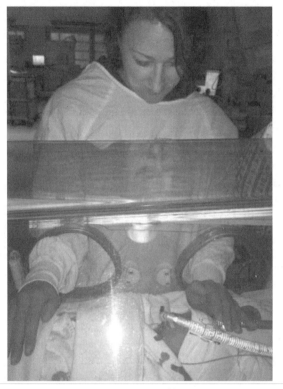

Kathy does Reiki on a preterm infant in the NICU

Reiki can only be used for positive purposes and can't harm in any way. It enhances and accelerates the body's healing ability and balances the chi.

Most people who practice Reiki are in the healing arts, but many lay people learn it to help with family, friends or personal development. Reiki is great for children, plants and animals. It can help with emotional healing after a loss or breakup, physical healing to speed the process and on a spiritual level to provide grounding or focus. I have used Reiki with great success on terminally ill clients to give them peace and a sense of healing in their final days and moments. It's a beautiful modality.

Reiki practitioners exist in practically every city in the world and are easy to locate on the Internet or in health-related publications.

If you are looking for a Reiki healing session, ask the practitioner how long they have been practicing and what level they have been taught. Some use crystals and other accouterments; ask what their healing involves in advance. Though it's not as important these days, people used to put great importance on whether they could trace their lineage to one of the original teachers. You should know, though, what the healer's background is and where they studied. Make sure you connect with them and trust them, or seek another healer.

If you want to learn Reiki, seek out a seasoned, Level III Master. Someone should not be teaching others without years of practice. Ask if your attunement involves a healing session first, which is how I practice, and if handouts are included. Also, make sure they can give you a certificate, especially if you want to be a practitioner yourself. You may want to meet the person before committing to the attunement and, if you don't feel a good connection, seek guidance elsewhere. There are now many versions of Reiki, slightly different symbols, different names, and different methods. A strict group believes Reiki should be exclusive and expensive. Others give hundreds of people attunements in a weekend at a campsite. For $75 you can become a Reiki Master on eBay. (Please don't do that.) Reiki is becoming more mainstream. Even hospitals and cancer centers are now embracing Reiki's healing, and research is being carried out on its success rates. I personally have seen it speed wound healing, help with broken bones, heal broken hearts and give my clients (and myself) a beautiful sense of peace and balance.

Pivotal Moments that made me who I am

We are all faced with a moment that changes the trajectory of our lives. It makes us a different person. Perhaps it's the birth of a child, the death of a loved one, a medical diagnosis or something as simple as a sunset. Through our lives these moments serve to define us and move us into a new iteration of ourselves. You will find these brief personal stories peppered throughout the book. Enjoy.

FROM BULLIED TO BILLBOARD

Billboard in Times Square, NYC

I was bullied. And teased. And picked on. And made fun of. I had few friends. I was embarrassed about almost every aspect of myself. No matter what I did, it was wrong. My best friends were the cafeteria ladies and the janitor. I spent many days in the nurse's office because I couldn't handle the teasing. I hated school. No, I loved school; I hated what happened to me there. Thank God for the teachers; they made it bearable.

From about 4th grade to 10th grade, I went through various times of intense teasing and bullying. People have a hard time believing this about me, but it happened. There was a girl in grade school who terrorized me for years. Hitting, slapping, tripping; she was very physical. Now, I think how sad must her home life have been that she learned to be that way. Starting in junior high it was the verbal abuse. Name-calling, paper-throwing, etc. I would come home every day and have to empty the wads of paper out of my jeans from people throwing them down the back of my pants in class. It was humiliating. I never told my parents. I was called horrible names, picked on for how I walked, talked, what I wore…or didn't wear. When I couldn't afford designer jeans, I was picked on for wearing off brands. And the following year when I proudly showed up in Jordache, I was asked who the hell did I think I was. If I didn't know the answer, I was dumb; if I did know the answer, I was a showoff. I couldn't win.

When I discovered drama club and the theatre, I finally found myself. I could be as weird and off-center as I wanted and no one cared. In fact, they were probably struggling with the same thing.

There was one day in 9th grade where randomly one of the girls on the bus announced she was going to kick my ass after school. I was stunned; she was my friend, wasn't she? I asked her why. "Because I want to" was her only answer. I said I wanted to read a book, and tried to convince her go that route. No dice. And every day for weeks she threatened this on the bus. And every day I would step off the bus and talk to the crossing guard until she got bored and walked away. But the day I dreaded arrived. I knew it would. The crossing guard wasn't there. I looked out the bus window and knew I was doomed. I thought I would puke. Now, I knew *how* to fight. I just found it pointless. I'm sure I could have whipped her, but I didn't see the need. We got off the bus and I was nauseous, sweating, terrified. My few friends sort of hovered about. They were the nerds and outcasts too; what could they do? I started up the long hill and she followed. She pushed me from behind and I said, "Look, I don't want to fight you." Too bad. Someone, another person I thought was a friend, shouted, "Throw her books down the hill." So she did. And the fight ensued.

I had the upper hand for a second. I had actually lifted her off the ground and was about to throw her down when she got her hand over my nose and mouth and I couldn't breathe. I let go of her and she pushed me down. And she and her friends walked away laughing.

My friends helped me up, gathered my books and we walked home. Silently. When everyone else had split off to their respective streets, my neighbor Julie asked if I was ok. I wasn't. I was scared and humiliated. I remember her holding my books as I blew my nose into the very stylish bandana I kept tied on my purse. "What if this happened every day?" I asked her. She had no answer. I arrived at my house, composed myself and went inside to see my sick mother. I never told her about the fight, about how scared I was. I couldn't. I never told my dad either. Actually, for anyone who wasn't there, they never heard the tale until now.

You may be wondering why this story is in things that changed my life. Well, my lack of friends, or perception of lack of friends, the judgment I felt, the lack, the inadequacy – this all made me who I am right now. Maybe it was that I had something to prove. I don't really know. But I do know that every experience shapes who we are. All that criticism helped form me today. And when I was on the billboard in Times Square in 2014, I had hundreds of comments on Facebook. From people who didn't ever speak my name in high school, threw paper down my pants and even…who beat me up. Yes, we're friends on Facebook. They were so proud of me, so excited. Told me I was the talk of the town, the best thing to ever come out of Penn Hills. And for just a fleeting second I wanted to say, "Fuck you." And then I realized I should really say, "Thank you." All that adversity made me strong. Well, stronger. Those people who challenged who I was made me who I am.

HERBS: NATURE'S PHARMACY

I started to have a fascination with herbs when I was in high school. It was one of the things that I had wondered about for my mom. When I moved to Los Angeles I discovered, much to my delight, that there was an herbal store right near my apartment.

At that point I was suffering from asthma and sinus issues and I thought herbs would be the way to go. I went to the store for the first time with glee and asked them what I could use to help me with these ailments. They explained that they were not allowed to prescribe, diagnose or recommend things to me so they handed me a book, *Today's Herbal Health* by Louise Tenney. I still own my original copy with binding broken and pages loose. I flipped through the book and found several things that might help me. I bought them in bulk and decided that I was going to make teas. I did that for a while then realized most of the teas tasted terrible. I went back to the herb store again and found out I could make my own capsules. They had a small device where you separate the capsules, put one half in little holes, fill them with the herbs and then top them with the other part of the cap.

It was at this point in my life that I assumed herbs were completely safe. They were natural, right? So I never considered that they could interact with other things, that you could take too much, or that you could have a negative reaction. As I was deciding which capsules to make, I saw a blurb in my herb book about horseradish and saw how great it was for sinuses. So, I bought a quarter of a pound of dried, powdered horseradish. Now you must remember my upbringing. I was not exposed to exotic food or anything "fancy" so I had no idea what horseradish was.

I got home very excited to solve my problem with my sinuses, made a bunch of horseradish capsules and happily took six.

Then the hell on earth started. My stomach was burning to the point where I thought I was going to die. I was screaming in pain, hunched over, clenching my abdomen, tears streaming down my face. My boyfriend handed me the gallon of milk. I drank the milk (well, guzzled down the milk). It helped for about ten minutes. I immediately sent him out for another gallon of milk, which I also guzzled. After several hours, the searing pain in my abdomen went away. You would've thought I learned my lesson from that. But apparently I was a moron. Or too trusting in the gentleness of nature. I decided that I had simply taken too many capsules, as it did indeed help my sinuses. It cleared up everything else in my body too. This time I was going to be smart, I decided I should only take three capsules. Idiot. Once again the burning ensued. Thank God I had more milk on hand and I learned my lesson about herbs.

Clearly, I didn't know much about herbs at that time in my life. I had worked with them a little bit with Dr. Pat way back in college and found a fabulous formula called BF&C, which I still use to this day. (There is a more information on that in the section of this book pg. 115)

When I started studying for my doctorate and PhD, I learned a lot about herbs, both Chinese herbs and American.

My threefold perspective on health is this: the first thing you want to do is to remove things that are causing problems. If you continue to do things that are bad for you, you can only understand that you're going to have issues. The second thing is to add back in things the body needs that you're not getting. Perhaps it's a specific vitamin or mineral or more water. Then the third thing is to put extraneous stuff on top. That's where herbs fall in. So where herbs were my go-to solution back then, now I don't use them very often. I found hops to be incredibly good for gas and indigestion. And chamomile for sleep, feverfew for migraines, valerian root for sleep and St. John's wort for depression.

But here's a perfect example of the ignorance that can surround herbs. Did you know that St. John's wort can negate the effects of the birth control pill? What a surprise. You're not depressed anymore until you get the pregnancy test results back. You want to be careful what you're putting into your body if it has any sort of chemical compound to it. Herbs are no exception. There are many great books available to talk about interactions and what herbs are going to be safe with pharmaceuticals and other herbs. Or check with a professional.

What follows is a brief introduction about different things you can do with herbs, tinctures, pills and infusions.

Herbs are a valuable source of natural medicine. Vitamins and minerals from herbs have been used safely for centuries. Many prescription drugs have their origins in herbal medicine. Aspirin, for example, is derived from white willow bark. The advantage of herbal medicine is that you get the whole compound, which often eliminates any side effects that might be present if it is broken down and turned into a prescription or over-the-counter drug.

There is certainly some overlap amongst herbal traditions but there is a large distinction between Chinese and American herbal therapy. Ayurveda (traditional Indian medicine) also utilizes an herbal system of medicine. There are many premade individual and combination herbal formulas so you don't have to feel responsible for concocting your own. It is important to remember that these *are* chemical compounds and may interact with other drugs or may need to be eliminated before surgery. Make sure you inform your medical team of any herbs that you are taking. You can also reference the book *A-Z Guide to Drug-Herb-Vitamin Interactions* (copyright 2006 by Healthnotes, Inc.). Like other natural health remedies, herbs encourage the body to heal itself and activate the natural powers that we possess. Here are some common ways to take herbs.

-Capsule: Gelatin capsule containing powdered or chopped herbs that are typically unpleasant to take directly by mouth. Most commercially available herbs are given this way.

-Compress: A pad or cotton dipped in herbs that have been boiled in water. Good for swelling, pain, etc.

-Infusion: Pouring hot liquid over the herb, steeping and drinking as a tea.

-Poultice: Warm mashed or ground herbs applied directly to the skin.

-Tincture: Another common way to find commercially prepared herbs; this involves soaking the herbs in an alcohol base, straining them, then taking the extracted liquid by mouth or using externally. This is a convenient way to take the herbs. They have a long shelf life with this preparation, as the alcohol preserves the herbs. You can also buy herbs in bulk and make your own tinctures at home.

To make your own tinctures, take an ounce of whole or cut herbs and put in a glass container with a lid. I recommend glass instead of plastic since plastic can leach into the tincture. Cover the herbs with alcohol – I typically use vodka. Put the lid on and shake twice daily for two weeks. Strain the mixture and bottle the liquid.

The method you use to take herbs is entirely up to you and what is available in your area. Most cities now have an herbal shop where you can buy herbs in bulk and take them any way you'd like. Some do have a less than desirable taste and may be better in capsules or tinctures. Many garden stores have potted herbs that you can grow at home and you can probably find seeds for most common herbs online. If you want to make your own teas, empty tea bags are available that you stuff and seal with an iron. You could also use a tea ball commonly found in kitchen stores.

If you'd like to make your own capsules, this is easy to do as well. I recommend getting the herbs in powdered form or using a coffee grinder to make the particles smaller. You can either put the ingredients in a bowl and just fill and close the empty capsules, or you can get a capsule maker, which is affordable and readily available online. They typically hold 25 or 50 capsule halves. You pour the herbs across the tops until the half capsules fill. Then, place the other half on top to seal the capsule. It sounds complicated, but it's easier to use this when making a lot of doses.

Capsule maker

There are some good herbal books available and online resources abound. Remember to double check your sources, make sure the herbs won't interfere with any prescriptions and know that herbs are chemicals and will react in the body, so don't assume they are safe just because they are natural.

As a side note: many people self-prescribe when it comes to herbs. While in most cases that is safe, I recommend doing in-depth research, talking to a professional herbalist or health practitioner or taking herb classes.

HOMEOPATHY: A LITTLE SUMTHIN', SUMTHIN'

〰️

H omeopathics have been an interesting part of my alternative medical life. I didn't know much about them until I moved to California and discovered the joy of Arnica. It's really fascinating in that everything I came to incorporate into my practice I learned from other people, who oftentimes just mentioned something in passing. But now homeopathics are definitely a part of my daily toolbox, even more so than herbs. I discovered that Gelsemium was my go-to homeopathic if my throat started to hurt. It took away any feeling of something coming on. And you can't beat the combination Oscillococcinum by Boiron if you think you're getting the flu.

The great thing about homeopathics is it treats *your* specific symptoms in *your* specific body. If twelve people went to the doctor complaining of headaches, usually the majority of them would walk out with the same prescription and diagnosis. Whereas with homeopathy you might walk out with twelve completely different remedies. Homeopathy works with very specific symptoms. In fact, the more specific and unusual, the better it is to find a remedy. For example, let's go back to that headache. If it only hurts on the right side and your right cheek is flushed and you feel like you want open air and it hurts more when you lie down, that is going to lead you to a specific remedy. A headache that takes up the entire head that feels better after you drink water, and that hurts more when you bend over is going to lead to a completely different remedy.

Homeopathics are probably one of the most controversial substances in alternative medicine. And I have seen on forums where people's comments have been, "I really believed what she was saying until she told me she believes in homeopathics, and with her promoting that bunk, I know she's a quack." It's really a shame, because in terms of our Western medicine, there are so many methods of alternative medicine that are completely misunderstood or not understood very well that are extraordinarily productive and effective for people to use for their health.

Dr. Samuel Hahnemann, who did most of his early tests on himself, discovered homeopathic medicine. He proposed the theory of "like cures like," meaning a compound that in a high dose causes a problem, in a low dose will take care of the problem. It's like the concept of a vaccine but using natural plants, compounds and minerals.

Whereas Arnica is definitely one of the most common, another one of my favorites is Nux Vomica, which is great for overindulgences of all kinds. Not just alcohol but also food and excitement. I have seen situations where children get so excited about what they're doing they are practically making themselves sick. This is a perfect time to use Nux Vomica. I have also used it for bouts of food poisoning. On one of my first trips to Las Vegas for a conference, I found myself eating with a colleague at one of the buffets. Unfortunately, I chose the seafood. Bad choice. I woke up at about four o'clock in the morning vomiting violently and feeling incredibly ill. I waited until about six and called my newfound friend, who happened to be a homeopath. I begged him to bring me some Nux Vomica. He did more than that: he raided the exhibit hall and brought me multiple homeopathic compounds and also the Western options of Pepto-Bismol and Alka-Seltzer. From that point on I have always traveled with Nux.

Here is a little bit of the history of homeopathics and how they can be used. I've also included some information about homeopathics for children. This is a great option for kids and animals, as there are typically no side effects and there are no ill effects of using this medicine. It comes down to this: it is affordable to try, there are no side effects and the worst thing that could happen is that it doesn't work. I encourage people to give homeopathics a try. If you go to your health food store and buy one of the little single remedy vials, please understand that the conditions that are imprinted on the side are merely suggestions and homeopathics can be used for multitudes of illnesses and issues.

What is Homeopathy? Hopefully this will clear up the mystique.

The American Heritage Science Dictionary defines homeopathy (hō'mē-ŏp'ə-thē) as "A nontraditional system for treating and preventing disease, in which minute amounts of a substance that in large amounts causes disease symptoms are given to healthy individuals. This is thought to enhance the body's natural defenses."

Classical Homeopathy involves comprehensive questioning and analysis of a patient's symptoms and physical, emotion, spiritual responses to each disorder. For example, a headache would be examined in regard to what brought it on, what makes it better or worse, is there a time of day that aggravates it? Is it limited to a certain part of the head, what were the circumstances that caused it, etc.? Classical homeopathy is used most often to treat a specific disease or symptom. In this type of practice, one remedy at a time is given. It's thought that the combination remedies commonly found in drugstores are less effective, if effective at all.

Constitutional Homeopathy treats the root personality of each patient. It can be described as a remedy, which covers the totality of a patient's mental and physical characteristics over a long period of time, excluding temporary changes during an acute illness. Constitutional homeopathy, in contrast to classical, is not necessarily used to treat a specific symptom, but to balance the whole being and promote homeostasis. There is a belief that we cannot actually change constitutions but that we can become healthier, more positive versions of it.

Regardless of what type of homeopathy you are utilizing, the correct remedy is determined by an in-depth interview or a questionnaire. The prescribing therapist may ask you more probing questions about the symptoms, your childhood, your parents, etc. It is not always easy to find the correct remedy, but when it is selected, a change can be seen almost immediately. Didier Grandgeorge, in his book, *The Spirit of Homeopathic Medicine* (1998), states, "For each homeopathic remedy we have tried to find **the dominant idea** representing the problem that the individual is confronting at the unconscious level. By studying in this way the whole range of physical and mental symptoms of an ill person, we discover the homeopathic remedy that covers the totality of symptoms."

It's not just enough to choose the right remedy. The dosage is just as important. If you are self-prescribing and buying the medicine in the store, you will either get a combination remedy or a very low dose (30X or 30C). By law in the United States, the higher potencies are only available through homeopathic practitioners. Some diseases react better to different potencies and it's important to discuss what the dosage will be, how often you should repeat it, and what do to if the symptoms return or new symptoms appear.

Most homeopaths believe that certain substances will counteract the effect of the medications. Coffee, camphor, toothpaste and marijuana should not be used while you are taking homeopathics. They also recommend waiting 15 minutes before eating or drinking anything. Also, most practitioners will encourage patients to stop any prescription medications if possible. This can cause problems, as most allopathic physicians don't understand or acknowledge the value of homeopathics. Try to be open with your doctor, though, and don't ever stop medication without alerting them first.

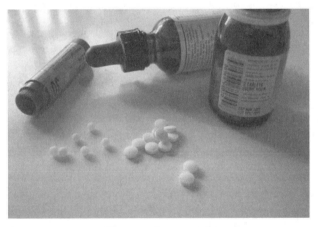

Choices in homeopathy

Homeopathic medications come in several forms: liquid, sugar pills and lactose pills. You never want to handle the medicine; either drip the liquids into water or your mouth (don't touch the dropper with your lips), and, with the pills, empty the correct amount into the cap and then put straight into your body.

Homeopathy is not a "one size fits all" system of medicine like we see in our prescription-happy Western practitioners. Through the use of the above-mentioned interview and questionnaire, the practitioner can find the remedy that is right for you. Two people could come into the office, both feeling depressed, and walk out with two very different, perhaps opposite, remedies. If the first remedy you are given doesn't work, another remedy is available for you to try. Homeopathic practice builds a relationship between patient and doctor; there is a lot of communication and trust formed through this type of medicine. Through using Homeopathics, physical dis-ease can be treated as well as emotional and spiritual issues; symptoms are not just covered up as in Western medicine.

The benefits of homeopathy are numerous. One benefit is that there are no adverse side effects as there can be with prescription medication; thus it is totally appropriate for children, pregnant women, even pets. The patient may have a temporary worsening of symptoms while the body adjusts to the remedy but this is usually fleeting. In some cases, the patient may even experience old symptoms in reverse order, thus clearing the whole body. For example, the asthma may clear, but the sinus problems from years ago may return, then go away, then the old eczema will return, until all ailments are resolved and true healing occurs. This is a positive sign, as symptoms disappear in the order they showed up. They should also move from inside out, so the stomachache may resolve, but old skin problems might show up temporarily.

Another benefit is that homeopathy is individualized medicine exclusive to each patient, which is in direct contrast to Western medicine.

Other benefits include the affordability of the substances. The remedies are quite affordable and abundant. According to Grandgeorge, "One single gram of mother tincture of Arnica provides enough Arnica 15 CH to treat the entire human race."

Another advantage is that homeopathy can produce lasting change in the body. It is not a temporary cessation of symptoms; it helps the body truly heal itself. Though it is easy to find combination remedies in health food stores – for example, a tube might be labeled simply PMS or headaches – these are formulated with the most common remedies that treat that ailment. Only one or two might be really needed. It's recommended to see a qualified practitioner to get the specific homeopathic that will address your exact needs.

If you want to work with homeopathics for your family, first I suggest writing down everything that is going on with the illness. Here are some things you will want to know:

<u>How did it start?</u> Gradually, suddenly, after exposure to cold, etc.

<u>Where does it hurt, specifically?</u> Not just "my head hurts," but what part of the head? The more detailed the better.

<u>What does it feel like?</u> Is it heavy, scratchy, burning, and itchy? Is it on one side of the body more than the other? Once again, the more descriptors the better.

<u>Is there discharge?</u> What does it look like? Is it copious? Watery? Yellow? Discharge is an important key to what the body is doing and helps you find a remedy.

<u>What personality signs are showing with the illness?</u> Is the person suddenly clingy, angry or pouty? Note what behaviors are different than normal.

<u>Is there anything bizarre?</u> Does he/she have irregular cravings, like an extreme desire for cold liquids, or exhibit strange behavior, like crying until put into a bathtub? In homeopathy, sometimes the most bizarre symptom is the one that clues you in to the right remedy.

Now that you have written all that down, you need to find the right remedy. There are great homeopathy books on the market that key you in to the right remedy, and there are also remedy finders online. I like the books *Everybody's Guide to Homeopathic Medicines* by Cummings and Ullman, *Homeopathic Medicine for Children and Infants* by Ullman, or *The Spirit of Homeopathic Medicines* by Didier Grandgeorge. There are sections for children and also most adult ailments and they give you ideas of what information you will need for each symptom. Once you find the right remedy, head to your local health food store and buy it. They are very affordable and because you use so little of it, it can last a long time.

Here is an example for you. A child comes home with an earache. He is craving physical contact and wants to be held. He wants fresh air, is not thirsty at all and there is yellow discharge from the ear and nose. This leads to the remedy **Pulsatilla**. Another child is in the later stages of an earache. She's weak, tired and whimpers, but is not as interested in physical contact. She's chilly and likes being under warm blankets but her hands, feet and head are sweaty. The remedy for her would be **Silica**. (I found this information in *Everybody's Guide to Homeopathic Medications*, mentioned above.)

If this sounds too complicated for you, there are other options. One is to consult a homeopathic practitioner in your area. They will take down the signs and symptoms and give you the right remedy. Another option is to use a combination remedy that is available in most health food stores. Companies take the most common remedies for any given ailment, combine them all together and sell them that way. They have combination remedies for everything from teething to PMS. A combination remedy I recommend for the flu is Oscillococcinum; it works best when you feel the first hint that illness is coming on. As I mentioned, homeopathics are available in sugar tablets, lactose tablets and liquids. They are all just as effective; choose the one that works for you or is most readily available. Your health food store professional can point you in the right direction and often they have books available there that you can look through.

I encourage you to explore this classical system of medicine and experiment to see if it might help you and your family.

GO WEST, YOUNG LADY

I t was my dream after I graduated college to move to Los Angeles and pursue an acting career. I graduated in June 1992 and on December 12 of 1992 I had everything I owned packed into a U-Haul strapped to the back of my Buick Century, ready to drive cross-country with my boyfriend. It was a hell of a summer. I did two shows, worked two jobs, and came down with mono. I was exhausted, stressed, overwhelmed, but excited to get my life started in Los Angeles. These were the days before Google, the Internet and Craigslist, so I went to Los Angeles with about $1800 to my name, no job and an unseen apartment that I found from an LA Times that my father ordered for me. I knew a total of ONE person in LA. I had asked a few of my actor friends in Pittsburgh who had previously lived in LA what areas were safe. I ended up choosing North Hollywood. Right on Lankershim Boulevard, which seemed a combination of Mexico and Monroeville. (For those of you who don't live in Pittsburgh, I know that reference makes no sense.) It had a swimming pool and it was a teeny little studio and it was heaven. I then quickly acquired another dream, my first cat. And followed that up with a rabbit because I was an idiot.

The drive cross-country was exciting but there was also a bit of trepidation and fear about starting a new life. I don't remember being as nervous about it as I probably should've been. I think because I always had it in my mind that that's what I was supposed to do, it seemed completely easy for me. Now I look back at the event and I think how brave I was for actually taking the leap and moving across the country knowing hardly anyone. And with no job. I got hired pretty much immediately at the local IHOP. I didn't even know what IHOP was because we didn't have those in Pennsylvania. I worked as a waitress until one of my regular customers offered me my first office job. I became an account executive and was making more money and got to wear real clothes. And I wasn't covered in syrup.

My life in LA grew from there. From day job to day job, acting gig to acting gig. I got some stellar rolls in some my favorite stage shows like *Little Shop of Horrors* and *Philadelphia Story*. I did commercials, a little bit of TV and some independent films. But stage was my favorite. And now looking back at this move oh so many years ago, I applaud my bravery: my bravery for taking charge of my life, leaving my family and friends, driving to a completely unknown place, knowing no one, with hardly any money. I applaud the chances I took, the risks I took and I know it was that type of behavior that led me to the phenomenal life I have now. Again I say GO FOR IT. If you want to drive cross-country and be an actor, go for it. If you want to travel to Alaska, go to Egypt to see the pyramids, jump out of an airplane, save your money, shore up your nerves and go for it.

BACH FLOWER ESSENCES: HE CAN CALL ME FLOWER IF HE WANTS TO...

I can't remember how I discovered the joy of Bach Flower Essences but I have used them for my clients, my pets and myself for years. You might know of this system of healing from the very popular Rescue Remedy. It's a combination of flowers that is good for relieving stress. I carry Rescue Remedy in my car and my purse. And it has gotten me through near car accidents, a knife in my hand, a divorce, two weddings, multiple funerals and a few acceptance speeches. It is one of the best remedies that I have found for stress in an acute situation. Rescue Remedy isn't meant to be taken over long periods of time, however. For that, it's recommended that you get a customized formula. You can do it yourself but I recommend a professional make them for you.

The history of Bach Flower Essences appears below. But suffice it to say it is one of the most useful non-toxic things you can do for your body and your mind. It doesn't actually affect our physiology, it works purely on emotions. After years of someone pounding on your emotions, whether it's an abusive boyfriend or an alcoholic father, Bach Flower Essences can be used to put everything back in balance. I have found this useful for things like low-grade depression, anxiety, jealousy, an overbearing attitude toward the family and dozens more. Usually a combination of these essences is made following a health consultation and a questionnaire being filled out. You take a mother bottle of the remedies (main bottle), mix it all together, add water and there you go. Healing in a bottle.

For those of you interested in the history of the remedies, here it is. In the 1930s, Edward Bach, a medical doctor and bacteriologist, discovered Bach Flower Essences. He used 38 individual flowers plus a combination of five flowers he called *Rescue Remedy*. Dr. Bach's healing theories were cutting edge for the time. He believed that every person had the ability to heal him- or herself and that anyone could use the flower remedies. He chose plants with high vibration and expected them to heal through that vibration. He ignored physical symptoms, instead focusing on disharmonies of energy. To him, the principles of unity, perfection and harmony meant more than disease, dysfunction and sickness. Dr. Bach's healing strategy was "Don't fight it, transform it," and he achieved that through his simple remedies.

The essences work on the emotional state of the person, transforming the negative into positive. These negative states can lead to disease and, though Bach Flower Essences don't address physical issues, they can stave off illness through balancing the spiritual/emotional state. They are homeopathically prepared, which means there is no *chemical* aspect of the plants left. They work strictly on a vibrational level.

Bach Flower consultation

To use the remedies, typically the client fills out a questionnaire and the chosen remedies are determined by those answers. I equate this to the keys on the piano. We are all born with emotional "notes." From someone pounding on certain keys, such as an alcoholic father, abusive stepparent, mental illness in the family, early losses and such, those events bang on the keys and they get out of tune. Flower essences come in and retune our emotional piano.

The chosen essences are mixed into a master bottle and will be taken four times a day. It's not recommended to use more than seven flowers at a time. Often the emotions unfold like an onion and as you balance some emotional states, different ones will appear. It's good to reevaluate the formula after a few weeks and change what's necessary. I've noticed that people will just suddenly stop taking the remedy or lose it. That seems to be an indication that a new formula is needed.

There are numerous advantages to Bach Flower Essences:

-You get quick results. I've seen change in a matter of hours. Rescue Remedy works very quickly and has gotten me through numerous crises (see above). It's good stuff!

-They are affordable. Each remedy costs about $14 and can be found at health food stores and online. You can also purchase the full series of remedies to mix for yourself and others. That runs between $415 and $465, depending on whether you want the stylish leather case or not.

-If it doesn't work, there are no side effects. It simply won't do anything.

-The essences don't interact with other meds or therapies, though you should still tell your physician you're taking them. (Their expression is priceless).

-You can do it yourself, though the input and expertise of a trained professional is always recommended.

-They are great for kids and pets. I had a client who used Rescue Remedy for her nervous horse; she would just put it in his water. They now make alcohol-free Rescue Remedy for pets and kids. If alcohol is a problem for you, place in warm water to evaporate the alcohol.

-This is customized medicine, not one-size-fits-all therapy. There are millions of combinations that could be made from those 38 flowers. For example, there are at least five different remedies that can be chosen for depression, depending on the cause and type.

When I recommend Flower Essences for clients, I have them fill out the questionnaire. I review their answers, ask more questions and try to determine what the best combination will be for them. I mix the formula and give them a handout that tells them what flowers are in the formula, what conditions they are being used for, directions on how to take it and I also include empowering statements or affirmations. I often recommend certain activities like gardening, deep breathing, walking or vigorous exercise, depending on the symptoms and the formula. (See example form below.)

The consultation can be done over the phone, but in person is better to observe body language and physical reaction during the interview. I follow up with the client in a few days and we reevaluate in two weeks. Usually I change the formula at that time.

Excerpt from real protocol.

Centaury: Neglecting your own needs and difficulty saying no (what the flower is for.)

Anytime anyone asks for something, ask "what are their real motives? And what do I really want?" (The first phrase is a recommendation, the next are affirmations.)

"I am solely responsible for my own development."
"I stand up for my own needs."

Elm: Overwhelmed

Provide more breaks when planning your work
"I am up to the situation."
"I always have the help I need."

Oak: Sense of duty, neglect own needs

Do exercises for neck and shoulder area
"I shall do it."
"Energy is flowing to me from the primal source."

Dr. Bach's essences are not the only ones out there; there are other similar protocols to be found. Australian Bush Flowers are another popular group that uses between 65 and 69 essences from Australian flowers. I found others that were invented and mixed by individuals. Practitioners can range from the self-taught to the "channeling the counsel of elders" to licensed and formally taught homeopaths and other natural health practitioners.

To learn about this system, there are Bach Foundation-approved courses that are taught in locations around the United States and also distance-learning opportunities. There is also an endless supply of books written on the subject.

The Keys to Unhealthy Living: The 'How to Stay Sick' List

I believe that we have enormous power for our own healing. Our choices affect our outcomes.

So…if you want to stay sick, here's how.

Back by popular demand from my other books.

Tell everyone you meet how horrible your life is. Make it an identity instead of an anecdote.

Find other negative people and make them your best friends.

Blame luck for everything; then you have no personal responsibility.

Say "Why me?" a lot.

Live in the past, think a lot about the bad stuff and tell everyone.

Fear the future. You know it's going to suck!

Ask for things that will help you and then ignore them or do them halfway.

Don't relax; after all, you're very busy.

Make excuses like: after the kids leave home, when I'm older, I'm too old….

Believe that what you think has no effect on the body.

Believe your illness/sickness is hereditary and you have no control.

Take no risks to grow and evolve.

Never laugh. It's for idiots.

Resent people from your past and blame them for who you are now.

Put yourself down at every turn. You truly are all those things you say.

Tell everyone how useless you are and use words like "never" and "always."

Blindly take every prescription that your doctor gives you, assuming he has your best interest at heart.

Surround yourself with negativity by watching the news and reading the paper often.

Don't stretch, eat right, breathe, drink enough water, poop, exercise or get any bodywork done.

Eat too fast when you are stressed and upset, and don't chew.

Remember there are never EVER options for the future.

Stay in a job you don't like, or with a spouse you can't stand.

Ask to be cured and not healed.

Envy everyone else for what you don't have.

Consume a lot of chemicals in food, water, air and home products.

Focus on all your problems.

Try to live up to what others think you should be, ignoring your own goals and desires.

Apologize for existing.

Let fear guide you and keep you stuck.

Hold on to your anger and negative emotions.

Try to fix everyone else; they're broken.

***Remember, you can never change!

A Better Choice: The 'How to Stay Healthy' List

Tell people of your successes and accomplishments. They can learn from you.

Find positive, supportive people and leave the negative behind you.

Take personal responsibility.

Know that others have bad times too; you're not alone.

Live in the present moment. Don't dwell on the past or be fatalistic about the future.

Go forward into the future with a positive attitude. It's going to be phenomenal.

Take risks to grow and evolve.

When you are gifted with something you asked for, be thankful and follow through.

Don't use words like "never" and "always."

Relax. Whatever that means to you.

Don't make excuses. The time is now.

Know that what you think has profound influence on your body.

You don't have to be your heredity. Perhaps there is another choice.

There are always options for the future.

Find a way to remove yourself from bad situations like jobs or partners. Or at least, change your attitude.

Laugh.

Don't blame or resent people from your past.

Know that healing comes from forgiveness and moving forward.

Check into your prescriptions before you take them. Do your own research.

Take a "news fast" and let the paper and newscasts go for a few days.

Stretch, eat right, drink enough water, have healthy bowels and have bodywork done.

Eat slowly, in a calm environment, and chew your food thoroughly.

Find true healing; don't just rely on a cure.

Take a high-quality multivitamin and mineral supplement.

Avoid GMO food.

Love deeply and feel greatly.

Speak only positively about yourself.

Eat real food and avoid processed and boxed products.

Tell the government and companies that supply our food that we want real ingredients and additives to be labeled.

Keep a food diary or try an elimination diet to see if your food might be affecting your health.

Know you have it within your power to change. At the very least, change your own mind.

And of course, GO FOR IT.

TAKING THE LEAP

Rafting in Oregon, the 15 ft. waterfall, Kathy in front row

My husband and I were taking a visit up to Portland, Oregon, and we decided to take advantage of some white water rafting, a sport that he and I had both enjoyed before. During this particular trip there was a section of the rapids that could not be rafted. You would get out of the raft, they would send the raft down through this very rocky area and then we would get back in the raft. There was a choice to be made, however, which was to jump off a 20-foot cliff into a standing pool of water and then swim to the raft or walk through the woods for a couple hundred yards and then get back on the raft. The guide asked who would want to jump. My hand immediately shot up and my husband shook his head no. A few others shook their head no but there were some takers to jump off the cliff.

There was a very "manly man" who wanted to go first. He posed at the edge of the cliff and asked his wife if he looked manly. I wanted to ask him what his father did to him but he jumped off looking completely manly and swam over to the raft. I decided that I would go second. The trick to this was you weren't allowed to run and jump, you had to stand on the edge and just jump out. But you had to make sure you put yourself in the center of this pool because the sides sloped down and there was a chance that you would whack yourself and be injured. That scared me a little bit as I didn't feel like paralysis was going to be very well managed in my future. I stood at the edge and my mind said, "Go ahead, go ahead," and my body said, "Oh hell no, oh hell no." I stood there vacillating back and forth trying to propel my body off this cliff and I finally stepped back and said, "Do you mind if I have a second? I'd like to try it later." He said, "Sure thing" and moved on to the other boy who decided he was going to jump. After he jumped, the guide said, "Okay, let's the rest of us walk along the path." I stopped him and said, "Wait, I want to try it again." He looked stunned. I walked up to the edge, turned to him and asked if it was okay to swear. He said sure and with that I flung myself off the cliff and landed with a splash in the water, yelling a very loud "Shiiiiiiiiiitttt" the entire way down. I hit the water, which was icy cold (I hadn't taken that into consideration), and actually went so deep my bottom hit the bottom. People cheered and I swam over to the raft where I was met with high-fives and "Atta girl"s. But I didn't do it for them. I did it for me. Once the guide had led everybody else back to the raft, he explained that nobody had ever gone back and actually done it again. If they couldn't do it the first time, they couldn't do it at all. And that he was incredibly proud of me. I was proud of me. I did this for nobody but myself. Why would I not stretch myself, to propel myself forward literally and figuratively into something that scared me? I was very proud of that moment. And felt that I had overcome a barrier to living. Sometimes you just have to jump right in with both feet.

NUTRITION: CHEAP, FAST AND EASY

If you are what you eat, then I spent most of my life being boxed, packaged, premade, filled with preservatives, additives and artificial flavorings and lukewarm. I ate at drive-thrus, usually in my car, or bought from 7-Eleven, and consumed in a stressful and unhealthy way. This was my life growing up and as an actress in Los Angeles. I remember times when all three of my meals would've been purchased at a gas station or other fast food-type establishment. It got to the point where if the food didn't have a steering wheel in front of it, I didn't know how to eat it. I got very good at maneuvering tacos and burgers and beef jerky while driving with my knees, putting on makeup and changing my clothes for an audition.

My mother, bless her heart, was not the greatest cook. What she made for my father and me back in the 1970s was packaged and processed. I loved Hamburger Helper night and she would treat me by giving me a couple spoonfuls of the beef before she mixed it with the noodly, powdery mixture. We lived off ham steak and boxed macaroni and cheese, jarred spaghetti sauce that had nothing in it because I didn't like chunks of stuff. Iceberg lettuce with Italian dressing and vegetables that were boiled till they looked like mush. In high school I lived off things like M&Ms and Mountain Dew and that translated to college, but I moved up the ranks to living off Mountain Dew and Reese's Peanut Butter Cups. I was dancing, at that point, five days a week, and I was thin and everyone assumed I was perfectly healthy, but I'm sure I was horribly malnourished.

When I moved to California, things just got worse, as if that was possible. I was dashing from audition to audition, leaving work and driving 45-90 minutes to do theatre. I learned that eating in the car was a convenient way to save time and money. I didn't have much of either. I remember friends of mine and myself driving way far away to do a show we were in and pooling our money in hopes we could get an extra taco at Taco Bell. We didn't have much money and we acted as a commune, supporting each other depending on who got paid that week. I remember specifically being in a show with a phenomenal woman named Verna. Someone was going next door to get sandwiches for the cast and I was asked if I wanted anything. I said no no no and shook my head. But Verna just looked at me. She knew, she could tell I didn't have any money. She ordered me a sandwich and took me aside later. She asked if I had any money and I said no. She said, "You do not ever deny yourself food. You are surrounded by people who love you who will always help you out. You don't ever *not* eat because you don't have five dollars."

Those times stick with me and I remember when I seriously didn't have five dollars to get a sandwich. Now I get to eat in fancy restaurants, I enjoy good food and wine with my husband and my friends or just myself. But it wasn't that long ago that I was scrounging for change in my car and hoping to get an extra taco with my dinner. Those days were not far behind and could always live in front of us too. We never know where our paths will take us. But I digress.

So, with my penchant for Mountain Dew, artificial sweetener in my iced tea and food that came from drive-through, how in the world did I give that all up and lecture around the country talking about nutrition? Though I looked thin, I know I was not healthy. I had horrible bowel issues and often fought with tremendous stomach cramps that doubled me over. I had completely irregular bowel movements, my sleep habits were terrible, I had low energy and looked listless. I had boundless energy externally, but internally I was exhausted.

One day I decided that maybe artificial sweetener truly wasn't the best idea. And since we live in a country where apparently names escape us, we must name things by color. I was always a pink packet fan; the blue packet did nothing for me as I couldn't stand the taste and it didn't make the item sweet enough for me. I decided the pink was probably not good and suddenly we have this new one, a yellow packet made from real sugar, wasn't it? I decided to try that. Immediately I got a headache, my asthma increased and I decided that maybe artificial sweetener altogether was a bad idea. I did some research and discovered this great natural sweetener called Stevia (the green packet). It is now my thing. I use Stevia to sweeten my tea and have not touched artificial sweetener in about fifteen years. The one time I did grab a packet because I had left my bottle of Stevia at home I immediately had heart palpitations, felt uncomfortable, had racing thoughts and anxiety. I had a hell of an asthma attack that night too. I have sworn off artificial sweetener completely and encourage everyone else to do the same.

Here is some info about artificial sweetener:

Sweet'N Low® (saccharin)

bladder cancer, breathing problems, headache, skin eruptions, diarrhea, reactions in people allergic to Sulfa drugs. However, it is the safest of the bunch. And has been around the longest.

NutraSweet®, Equal®, Sugar Twin® (Aspartame)
cancer, hair loss, depression, dementia, headaches, dizziness, nausea, vomiting, fatigue, seizures, ***increased hunger!
Converts in the body to methyl alcohol
which converts to formaldehyde.
In 1988, 80% of the complaints to the FDA were about aspartame.

Splenda® (sucralose)
contains chlorine; GI issues, wheezing, coughing, depression, mood swings; only studied short term on animals.

So I'm living in Santa Barbara and trying to maintain better health and since I was in the health field I decided I should probably cut out fast food. I can actually tell you the last time I had a McDonald's hamburger. It was about 13 years ago and it just sounded good, you know? I was driving by anyway. I stopped in and I got a Big Mac, which used to be my favorite, some French fries, because those we know are straight from God, and probably iced tea. Might still have been Diet Coke at that point. I ate the hamburger and it tasted so good; how did I ever give that up? But... in about ten minutes this horrible taste rose in my mouth and I felt immediately nauseous. For the next two days I had a horrible stomach cramps and we can't even talk about what came out in the bathroom. That was my last McDonald's hamburger. I still occasionally have In-N-Out, Tommy's or Fatburger, because I believe strongly in the 80/20 rule. Let me explain.

I don't believe we can do anything 100%. There are certainly things we should try. If you have a severe allergy, you certainly do want to avoid that trigger 100% of the time, but for diet changes, which are not life-threatening, I think we have to be realistic in our expectations. My treats of drive-thru hamburgers are few and far between, but when I do choose to eat them, I *choose* to eat them and I do so with joy, peace and permission. To eat something with the feeling of guilt or self-flagellation will do nothing for your health at all. In fact, it will make it worse. And we can choose to eat them in moderation. One time I stopped at Tommy's (they put really good chili on their burgers...so good). Anyway, I was driving by and stopped in. I ordered a single burger with chili. That was it. No fries or anything else. It was my moderate treat because I wanted the taste and had done flying trapeze that day so I had definitely worked off those calories. As I was waiting for my food, three women came in. They were quite obese, bellies pouring over the stretch pants, just really, really big. And I watched what they ordered. Every one ordered a double burger... and fries with chili...and a giant soda. I'm not sure it even crossed their minds to share fries, just get a single burger or have water instead of soda. The calories they consumed are probably what most people have over the course of a whole day. Their choices, or lack of them, were clearly contributing to their weight issues. It was quite sad.

So, for my journey, here we are, the changes started to occur. One: no more artificial sweetener. Two: no more soda. Three: no more fast food, with the exceptions of when I very consciously choose to have it. And here I am healthier than ever. I found my sleep habits improved, my digestion was better, my bowel movements were regular. The only shortcoming I have now is I know I don't drink enough water. I live off my giant container of iced tea (mostly water, I justify) and in most pictures of me speaking you'll see it looming in the background. It is something I'm working on. And I think that's okay. We are all a work in progress with no one yet finding perfection.

Many of my lectures and workshops are on things we should add and subtract for better health. Through the course of my studies, and my personal journey of learning about food, I learned that certain things are unacceptable in my diet and I encourage you to adopt these as well. Besides the artificial sweetener, I think **high fructose corn syrup** is one of the detriments of our society. It again is something I've almost completely cut out, with the exception of occasional dollops of ketchup when I'm in a restaurant.

From what we can tell, there's a clear correlation between high fructose corn syrup intake and the rate of obesity in this country. I can't really blame the companies. They thought they had found a cheap alternative to sugar; it increases their bottom line. I do appreciate a bottom line. But now that the evidence has come out as to how bad it is for us, I applaud the companies like Welch's that are taking steps to remove it from their food. And I encourage you to remove it from your food as well. Please don't believe the propaganda. It is not natural and it is not as safe as sugar. It is making this country obese and diabetic. There is evidence that fructose suppresses Leptin (the hormone that gives the sensation of fullness) and causes a rise in triglycerides and insulin resistance. The rate of obesity and type 2 diabetes almost identically mirrors the rate of our HFCS consumption. (See chart below.) Studies also show that high fructose corn syrup contains mercury and the producers have admitted it. The real downside of this is that only certain manufacturers produce HFCS that contains mercury and there is no way to know which one.

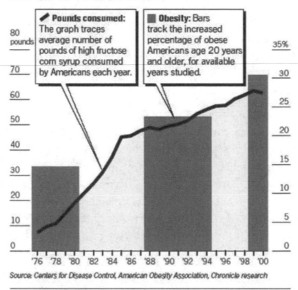

Obesity and high fructose corn syrup

The number of Americans who are obese has quadrupled in recent years, a study shows. At the same time, high fructose corn syrup consumption has risen at parallel rates.

Pounds consumed: The graph traces average number of pounds of high fructose corn syrup consumed by Americans each year.

Obesity: Bars track the increased percentage of obese Americans age 20 years and older, for available years studied.

Source: Centers for Disease Control, American Obesity Association, Chronicle research

Chronicle Graphic

Another huge controversy in this country is on **genetically modified foods**. I have been interviewed by major news outlets and have written countless articles on what I believe to be the detriment of genetically modified foods (GMOs or GMs). They have not been fully tested. I don't care who you ask, they have *not* been tested long-term on how they interact with all of our biologically individual bodies, and minds. Are GM products adding to allergies, gluten intolerance, obesity, mental health issues, anxiety and depression? We just don't know – and, personally, I do not want to be the poster child for the largest genetic experiment in the history of this world. None of us signed up for that.

For those people who say GM food is feeding the world, I asked them who are they feeding? Genetically modified foods go to the cheapest, packaged and processed products. We are not genetically modifying our broccoli to have more vitamins or oranges to boost our immune systems. We are genetically modifying corn, soy, and cotton, things that are going to feed feedlot animals and go into high fructose corn syrup, soy protein, cotton seed oil and soybean oil. Many packaged and processed foods, with all those colorful labels on the market and not labeled organic, typically indicate that they are filled with GM crap. So if we are indeed feeding the masses, we're feeding them a bunch of shit. Pardon my vernacular. We are not upping nutrition or vitamin content, we're giving already poor and undernourished people less nutrition for less money. Other countries are denying our crops, they're dumping our food into the ocean, they don't want our products. So the question I'll pose again, who are we feeding? And if we are feeding people, what is it doing to them?

Let's talk about the nitty-gritty of genetically modified foods. Most genetically modified produce has been made so that it can be sprayed with high amounts of pesticides, herbicides and fungicides. It used to be that the farmer had to walk through rows of crops and spray each weed individually. Now with the GM seeds called Roundup Ready, as an example, they can take a crop duster or hose and spray the entire field with pesticide. You think we're not eating that? So even if you think genetically modified foods are perfectly safe for us, pesticides aren't. I can quote study after study showing how horrible pesticides are for our brain development and how they are leading to cognitive and mental issues in our children. I don't have children but I don't want yours to be disturbed by genetically modified foods either. Oh, and as a side note, the same companies that produce the pesticides are the same companies that are making the seeds. Hmmmmm....

Though we don't have to worry about much produce that has been genetically modified, conventionally grown food is lower in nutrition and more contaminated with pesticides, herbicides and fungicides. Here is the latest about the "dirty dozen" – those foods that should be purchased organic.

As of this writing, according to the Environmental Working Group (www.ewg.org), the "dirty dozen" are: apples, strawberries, grapes, celery, peaches, spinach, tomatoes, potatoes, pears, cherries, nectarines, sweet bell peppers and hot peppers. Each of these foods contained a number of different pesticide residues and showed high concentrations of pesticides relative to other produce items.

And here is an easy way to find GM produce:

Check out the little stickers on your fruits and vegetables.

Traditionally grown food (using pesticides herbicides, fungicides, etc.) will have a 4-digit sticker.

Organic will have a 5-digit sticker that starts with 9 and is also usually labeled as organic.

GM produce will have a 5-digit sticker and start with 8.

9 is fine; we hate 8.

There are dozens and dozens of things that various people recommend we do away with. Wheat, soy, trans fats; some people think we shouldn't be eating eggs or meat or certain types of products. This isn't a book on nutrition, however; it's a book on my journey and your journey. And because I've mentioned before that we are all biologically individual, you must find what foods do and don't work for you. I tried to be a vegetarian. I did everything right. I ate my legumes, I had a balance of protein, yet it did not work for my body. And as a side note, the *Eat Right for Your Type* book is a bunch of bunk. Many very well trained nutritionists have disproven that book. It's impossible that there are only four ways to eat and that all Type Os should eat the same way. Anyway, the bottom line is, if it works for you, try it. I am blood type A and according to that book, I should be a vegetarian. According to my body, I should not. I was dreaming about meat, I lost a lot of weight; I was paler than usual and had constant headaches. It did not work for me. If it works for you and you're healthy and well (truly healthy and well), then go for it.

We have to be our best health detectives. No one is going to help us know our bodies better than we ourselves can. I'll give you a few examples. One was a client of mine. I massaged him and his wife every other week for years and years. One night before his massage I asked him how he was doing. He expressed that he'd ended up in the emergency room the week before. I was concerned and asked why. He told me that he thought he was having a heart attack; he was having heart palpitations and felt really weak. The emergency room ran a bunch of tests, decided it was a panic attack and gave him the appropriate medication. He doesn't get panic attacks. We talked about his stress level and I tried to determine if he was more stressed than usual. Nothing was different. He went on his way after the massage and two weeks later when I saw him again, he again expressed that he had ended up in the emergency room. Again he thought he was having a heart attack and again they determined it to be a panic attack and gave him medication. So we started to talk. I asked him if anything was changed and he said, "No. Well, actually, now that I think about it, I was trying to be healthier so I stopped using the Equal (the blue stuff). I said, "Great, what are you using instead?" He said "Splenda (the yellow stuff). Isn't that healthier because it's sugar?" "Nope!" I advised him to cut out the Splenda. As soon as he did, the panic attacks stopped, he felt better and never ended up back in the emergency room. He was having a reaction. People in the emergency room were not going to figure that out.

The other example is a personal one. You know I like to use those. I found that I was starting to have asthma at weird times. Let me explain. Once I moved to Santa Barbara, I typically have asthma from October to January or February. But I was having the attacks at weird times of the year. I decided I needed to figure this out. So I started to chart when I was having attacks. I was only having them on weeknights. That's weird. It got weirder. I realized I was only having them on weeknights when I went back to my office. Even weirder, as I spend every day in my office. But I realized that on nights I went back to work, I would grab a handful of M&Ms out of the antique cut glass candy dish. But that didn't make any sense; I've been eating M&Ms my entire life. So I separated them out by color (my husband thought I was crazy), but what I learned was when I grabbed certain colors, those were the nights I had asthma attacks. The blue, the red and the orange did it to me. Clearly it was something in the dye. Again, this is nothing that my physician was going to help me figure out. I had to be my own health detective. And I encourage you to do the same.

The last story is about Christmas. Christmas should be a happy time. Where families get together and enjoy good food and good company. However, there was one Christmas that didn't end so well. With few exceptions I always offer to help in the kitchen. This year I was helping. As I stirred the creamed corn, I looked longingly at the juice that ran off the spoon. I love creamed corn. After the meal, I'm not an idiot; I offer to help clean up. That way you get to pick at all the leftovers. There was a large amount of sauce left in the bottom of the creamed corn pan. I picked up the serving spoon, took a giant slurp and maybe got about two kernels of corn; the rest was this fabulous sauce. We finished cleaning the kitchen, played a few games and at about eleven o'clock I went to bed.

At midnight I awoke with the worst headache I've ever experienced in my life. I actually looked around the room to see who had been beating me with a bat. Searing pain through both my eyes. I felt nauseous. I felt like I had to use the bathroom and I was burning up. Not from the heat in my inlaws' house in Fresno, but heat coming from inside myself. I went to the bathroom and hoped for vomiting or a bowel movement but none came. I stumble back to bed and finally got back to sleep. About an hour later I woke again, this time absolutely freezing, shivering, heart palpitations, racing thoughts. I thought I was dying. The headache was even worse; again I felt nauseous and ran to the bathroom. I finally vomited and had a bowel movement. Something very unusual for me at two o'clock in the morning. I again went back to sleep. I woke the next morning and turned to look at my husband in the twin bed next to me who popped out his earplugs and happily said, "Good morning." I said, "Get me Advil and an ice pack immediately."

By nine a.m. I was finally able to function. I was pale and exhausted and I looked like I had been beaten with a stick but I was able to emerge from the bedroom. My mother-in-law took one look at me and said, "Oh dear, what happened to you?" I asked her what she had put in the creamed corn. She ran through the ingredients: corn, butter, cream, cornstarch… MSG. I stopped her there. What!? Who in the world cooks with MSG at their house? She told me it was in the recipe.

I explained to her that MSG was an incredibly bad toxin. And then proceeded to take a survey of the rest of the people in the house. Several had migraines, some had leg cramps that forced them out of bed in the middle the night, several had nightmares, many had anxiety attacks and others complained that their asthma was worse. I printed out a form from the Internet that showed my mother-in-law all the horrible things that MSG can do. (See below.) And then we stole her bottle of MSG. She replaced it a few times and we continued to steal it. Finally, I believe she got the hint and there's been no more MSG in her house. She's taken it out of hers, and I advise you to take it out of yours. No, not everyone is as sensitive to MSG as I am. But because I got such a huge dose of it, I feel like it kicked me into high gear. My husband can typically have it with no problems.

Since that incident, I have discovered that certain packaged and processed foods have MSG. The big downside is, it does not have to be labeled unless it's 99.9% pure. So if you see MSG on the label you know there's a hell of a lot of MSG in it. Look at things like Doritos and Taco Bell hot sauce. Since MSG doesn't have to be labeled, you can sneak it into your food under code names like flavoring or seasonings or natural flavorings. See the list below of common names. MSG does occur naturally but it's when it's chemically made (typically genetically modified) and added to food that it seems to cause a problem. This is why so many people stay away from Chinese restaurants, though I actually don't think they use it much anymore. I had a certain problem with a certain sandwich from a certain store, (thanks, Jared), not knowing that they had soaked their peppers in water that had MSG. I think they arrive to their store that way so I'm not blaming them per se, but I did have a horrible effect from it. And it bothers me that they claim to be so healthy and portray their meals as health food. Same thing with diet soda. It's not a health food. But anyway, no more peppers for me from that certain restaurant.

MSG is one of the insidious secrets to hide in our food. At least high fructose corn syrup needs to be labeled. And I know we are all longing for the day that genetically modified products have to be labeled. Things are changing, and please remember: with every swipe of the barcode, you cast your vote. Also with the stocks that you buy. Be smart about your choices, do the best you can 80% of the time, and happy eating.

According to www.truthinlabeling.org

Names of ingredients that always contain processed free glutamic acid (MSG)

- Glutamic acid (E 620)[2]
- Glutamate (E 620)
- Monosodium glutamate (E 621)
- Monopotassium glutamate (E 622)
- Calcium glutamate (E 623)
- Monoammonium glutamate (E 624)
- Magnesium glutamate (E 625)
- Natrium glutamate
- Anything "hydrolyzed"
- Any "hydrolyzed protein"
- Calcium caseinate,
- Sodium caseinate
- Yeast extract, Torula yeast
- Yeast food, Yeast nutrient
- Autolyzed yeast
- Gelatin
- Textured protein
- Whey protein
- Whey protein concentrate
- Whey protein isolate
- Soy protein
- Soy protein concentrate
- Soy protein isolate
- Anything "protein"
- Anything "protein fortified"
- Soy sauce
- Soy sauce extract
- Anything "enzyme modified"
- Anything containing "enzymes"
- Anything "fermented"
- Anything containing "protease"
- Vetsin
- Ajinomoto
- Umami

Names of ingredients that often contain or produce processed free glutamic acid (MSG) during processing:

Carrageenan (E 407)
Bouillon and broth
Stock
Any "flavors" or "flavoring"
Natural flavor
Maltodextrin
Oligodextrin
Citric acid, citrate (E 330)

Anything "ultra-pasteurized"
Barley malt
Malted barley
Brewer's yeast
Pectin (E 440)
Malt extract
Seasonings

MSG Sensitivity Symptoms:

Cardiac

Arrhythmia
Atrial fibrillation Tachycardia/Rapid heartbeat/Palpitations
Slow heartbeat
Angina
Extreme rise or drop in blood pressure

Circulatory

Swelling

Gastrointestinal

Diarrhea Nausea/vomiting
Stomach cramps
Irritable bowel
Swelling of hemorrhoids and/or anus area
Rectal bleeding
Bloating

Muscular

Flu-like achiness
Joint pain
Stiffness

Respiratory

Asthma
Shortness of breath
Chest pain
Tightness in the chest
Runny nose
Sneezing

Urological / Genital

Bladder pain (w/frequency)
Swelling of the prostate
Swelling of the vagina
Vaginal spotting
Frequent urination
Nocturia

Skin

Hives (may be both internal and external)
Rash
Mouth lesions
Temporary tightness or partial paralysis
(numbness or tingling) of the skin
Flushing
Extreme dryness of the mouth / thirst
Face swelling
Tongue swelling
Bags under eyes

Neurological

Depression
Mood swings
Rage reactions
Migraine headache
Dizziness
Lightheadedness
Loss of balance
Disorientation

Mental confusion
Anxiety
Panic attacks
Hyperactivity
Behavioral problems in children
Attention deficit disorders
Lethargy
Sleepiness
Insomnia
Numbness or paralysis
Seizures
Sciatica
Slurred speech
Chills and shakes
Shuddering

Visual

Blurred vision
Difficulty focusing
Pressure around eyes

The last thing I wanted to mention as far as nutrition is soda. I'm anti-soda, though I used to be a big fan. I was a Mountain Dew gal. In 1993, I actually belonged to the Church of Mt Dew online. Not my proudest moment. I would go through about a six-pack every day or two. It was my breakfast as I ran out the door and I drank it all day from there. I would do diet soda if the restaurant didn't have my Dew because I didn't like the taste of the regular as much. From that point many years ago, I can't even tell you the last time I had soda. It's been, perhaps, a decade. People ask me how I stopped. I just...did. I realized after a few days without it that I didn't like it anymore. It was too sweet, made me feel weird and just wasn't working in my body. In my transition of health, I would say that went right before the switch out of artificial sweetener.

Because when I left soda, I had more tea.

Soda is not a healthy beverage. The sweetener is bad for us no matter diet or regular. As I mentioned previously, the artificial coloring and additives are bad for us. Many people can't handle caffeine or carbonation. And let's talk about phosphorus. Soda, mainly the dark soda, contains phosphorus. We need a little, but we're getting a lot. And what does phosphorus compete with? Calcium. And phosphorus wins. So, for young ladies who are building bone or women worried about osteoporosis, soda is a no-no. There is no good reason to drink soda. In fact, the reason soda fountains and pharmacies were together was soda was there to kill the taste of the horrible medicine you were about to consume. It wasn't meant to be a daily beverage. You want to lose weight? Cut out the soda, both diet and regular.

Thousands of books have been written about nutrition, in general and specifics. Listen to your body, make the healthiest choices for you. And enjoy what you are eating. Bring back the ritual, which is sharing a meal, even if it's just quietly by yourself.

CHIROPRACTIC: LET'S GET CRACKING

I started working with a chiropractor for a little bit when I was still living in Pittsburgh. One of the things my mother did do to try to help her back before she realized it was cancer was to go to the chiropractor. I was probably thirteen or fourteen years old. I remember him having me bend over and running his fingers along my spine to see if I had scoliosis and I remember he had these awesome spine-shaped pens. I held onto mine for the longest time, thinking I would never be able to find another one of those again. Little did I know they're everywhere. I don't remember much about the chiropractic adjustments from when I was a child, if he even gave them to me.

I do remember seeing my first chiropractor when I had moved to Los Angeles. I was starting to have very bad hip pain from all the waitressing that I was doing. I don't remember much about his adjustments but I do remember he had the teeniest feet I'd ever seen. He was a very rotund man always dressed incredibly well, but he had these teeny little feet that he put in his Italian loafers. I remember looking down through the face cradle and him cracking my neck to where I was almost looking at my own behind. It was a little shocking the first few times but I got very used to it. And he fixed my hip in about three sessions.

I tried a non-force chiropractor and it didn't do anything for me. He would touch spots and make this horrible grunting sound. I have clients who prefer non-force and there is a place for that, so do what works for your body. I am so flexible that I really do need the cracking adjustments to make any change in my body. Sometimes non-force practitioners use a

79

tool called an activator. I have found this to be useful for myself and for clients who can't have the "cracking."

My biggest use of chiropractic when I was living in Los Angeles came before I got on a plane to go back to Pittsburgh. I sat down in my office chair, sneezed and couldn't turn my head. I was getting on a plane in just a few hours and was desperate for relief. I looked in the phone book and found someone within walking distance, as I didn't have a car. I called and made an appointment. This man ended up being an angel to me. He not only stayed open for me, then he also drove me back to my office so I wouldn't have to walk after the adjustment. He did a phenomenal adjustment, I had great relief in my neck and when it came time to pay him, he said $25. I looked at him, stunned. We were in the middle of Beverly Hills. I knew his going rate was not $25. He asked if I had insurance. I said no. He asked if I made a lot of money. I said no. He said, "Aren't you getting on a plane to get married?" I said yes. He said, "It's $25. And until you tell me otherwise, it will always be $25." And it was for years.

He explained to me that he saw a lot of wealthy people every week who paid him cash. He felt that it was his responsibility to take care of people and it's not like he didn't need my money, but he didn't need it as much because others were basically funding my treatments. I have tried to be incredibly generous with my clients as well and have given several cancer patients, artists and teachers breaks in their fees because I can. And I feel I should.

When I moved to Santa Barbara and started my massage practice, I contacted a bunch of chiropractors to see if I could work with them, since massage and chiropractic is a great team for healing. After over a decade, one, Dr. John Craviotto, is still my chiropractor to this day. He and I have worked together as a team on many clients and have helped probably hundreds of people heal.

When I was hit by a car at the end of December 2010, the ambulance showed up and asked if they could take me to the hospital. I said "No, but can you take me to my chiropractor?" They didn't find it amusing. I did end up at his office within an hour after my accident. I was starting to get a little loopy and I could tell by the look on his face that he was concerned about me. He had never seen me out of control or scared. He X-rayed my hand, as that's what the car hit, looked at my neck, did some light manipulation, no real big adjustments, and sent me on my way. It was his care and the care of another massage therapist that helped me get through that dramatic event.

I owe my chiropractors, all of them, so much. As much as I love massage and it is my field, there are times that it's a structural issue and not a muscle issue. Often it's a sciatica problem where the SI joint is out of place or someone will feel like they have a knot between their shoulder blades and it is a rib that has been put out of place. My chiropractor can take care of all those things. If you find that you're starting to have pain that is nagging, try a chiropractor (someone who is reputable and/or recommended) to see if they can help you. I highly recommend that system of medicine and have found it to be invaluable in my own life and in the lives of my clients.

Fly Through
the Air with the
Greatest of Ease

P eople are fascinated that I do trapeze and the story of how and why I started. It was actually pretty funny. I had a brand-new client in my office; she had gone to my website and noticed that I do a wide variety of things in my field. She asked me if I had any time for fun. I said I absolutely do and went through the litany of things my husband and I have experienced: skydiving, zip-lining, spelunking, rappelling, swimming with sharks, scuba diving, swimming with dolphins, white water rafting, jumping off a cliff, as you read. She looked at me and said, "Geez, girl, what's left on your bucket list?" I explained that I didn't believe in a bucket list, but if there were things that were in my power physically, mentally, financially able to do, why would I not do them? She asked if there was anything left that I hadn't gotten to yet. I explained that the trip around the world would have to wait until I have more time and more money, but that I had always wanted to do flying trapeze. As the words came out of my mouth, I thought, "Oh crap, I guess I better go do that."

As she was changing after her massage, I went out to my computer and searched for a place that I could do flying trapeze. And I found it, in Santa Monica, California. I looked at the dates they were available and the days I was available and realized that Easter Sunday was my first chance. I went home and told my husband that what I wanted to do was leave Saturday morning to go to Lake Shrine and meditate, spend the night, go to the Magic Castle to have fun, and wake up the next morning to do flying trapeze. He said go ahead. I'm very lucky in that I have the support of an accepting spouse who encourages me to do these things I want to do. I made all the arrangements and waited with bated breath to try my first trapeze class.

I showed up to the school about a half hour early very excited and expectant. They thought I was crazy. I kept checking back in and saying, "I'm here I'm here." They got it. My instructor was amazing. She had just gotten off a tour with Cirque du Soleil; they wanted her back but she wanted to teach. There were ten of us in the class. I climbed the ladder for the first time, a bit winded, got to the 25-foot platform and stood there thinking, "What the hell am I doing?" It seemed very high, even though I was belayed in with safety lines. I stepped to the edge of the platform and they handed me what turned out to be an incredibly heavy bar. It was hard to hold onto it and not feel like you were being pulled out across the net. On the "ready," you bend your knees, and on "Hep," you do a little bunny hop off the platform and fly. Your first trick is called the knee hang. You hang your knees on the bar just like you would as a kid on any playground. I put my knees on the bar, I let my hands go and I reached toward the ocean. "Arch your back," they said. I arched so hard I cramped the back of both my legs. Luckily I was able to undo the cramp and not fall off the trapeze. I laughed to myself thinking, "Overachiever." I dropped down into the net with a whoosh. It does take a little bit of air out of you even though it was a pretty soft landing and I got in line to do it again.

About forty minutes into the class it started to sprinkle. The instructors look concerned. I was bummed, what does this mean? Do we need to cancel class? And that's exactly what it meant. I didn't get to try my catch, which is the point of the whole thing. The catch is the most incredible thing, from what I was told. It's the culmination of the whole class. I asked if maybe the rain would stop and we could continue the class. At that point it started raining harder. I asked if I could hang around for the next class in hopes that it went on without a hitch. They said it was full but if I wanted to hang around perhaps someone would cancel and a spot would open up.

I thought I would never get back down to do this if I didn't finish this class so I had better stay. What happened after that was I sat in the staff hut and watched them have a staff meeting. Then we told funny stories about adventures we have had and silly people on the trapeze. Christina, Christina, and Blaine. Thank goodness these were my first coaches, as they inspired me to keep going.

Anyway, the second class came, the rain stopped and it was full. I was totally bummed again. I would have to drive two hours home to Santa Barbara having not been able to do my catch. Christina was great; she whispered to me, "You're number 11," and let me stay in the class. I felt so much more confident this time; I climbed the shaky ladder, got to the top, I let go on the "Hep" and jumped out onto the sky. I made my catch and landed safely in Blaine's arms as he swung back and forth. I plopped down into the net ecstatic and hooked. It's no irony that their slogan is "Forget fear, worry about the addiction." Because that's exactly what happened.

I got home that night from class still high and explained to my husband that I thought this would be my new thing. And it has been. As of writing this I just finished my 100th class and I'm doing really complicated tricks now. I have worked through complicated countless tricks, an emergency room visit, a giant bruise on my leg I thought would never go away, and punching one of the catchers in the face. Sorry, Sean. I had the privilege of performing for the first time in the student show at Emerald City in Seattle. I also did my first layout and first swinging out of lines. Trapeze is a great way to keep reaching for new and harder goals. It thrills me!

Trapeze for me is a total parallel to life. You climb that ladder to something you want; you have no idea what's going to happen. You jump off with a little "Hep" and hope you're going to be safe. You stay in the present moment, listen to your calls and do your trick. If your mind wanders even for just a second, or you think to the future or the past, you lose your footing and fail. Or fall. You reach out and trust that the catcher will be there. But even if he's not, you fall gently into the net, safe and sound. I'm not saying everybody should run out and do trapeze. But do something that stretches your limits, do something that expands your consciousness. Try something out of the box. I now consider myself a trapeze artist. Maybe you want to be a dancer or a sculptor or an artist. Find your trapeze. I was doing a radio show when I was telling the host about all the things I have done and she asked me if I had a death wish. I said, "No, I have a life wish." I want to experience everything I can in this body on this planet at this time. It's our privilege to do so. Go fly free.

The Pelicano, photo by TSNY

The catch with Sean, photo by TSNY

Holding my set, photo by TSNY

Exercise: 5,6,7,8

When I was a kid there wasn't as big an emphasis on exercise as there is today. We didn't need the NFL to encourage Play 60. I think it's because, really, that's what we did when we had time. We were out playing football, riding around on our bikes, playing pretend games, chasing each other around the neighborhood. We still had recess and gym class. We didn't have the indoor distractions like video games and computers to keep us from going outside and playing. Even growing up back East, we lived on a dead-end street running around and "exercising."

Among adults it was a different story. It was the 1970s and '80s when we started to hear about Jane Fonda and her workouts, Jazzercise, and really using your body to its ultimate performance. I remember all the dads walking up and down the street as we played football, as the moms would stand there gossiping about what they noticed in the neighborhood. Our moms then were definitely not as active as the moms are today.

Kathy in ballet

Since I grew up as a dancer, that was my form of exercise; I never considered doing anything else. When I was in college I would go to the fitness room and work out only to keep my body in shape for dancing. When I left college and moved to Los Angeles, I was lost; I didn't know what to do for exercise. I thought running on the beach would have a romantic air to it and I took great pleasure in leaving my little apartment in North Hollywood and driving to Santa Monica to run on the beach, my headphones blaring Madonna as I watched the waves come and go as I exhausted my body.

Because of the dancing and genetics, I've always been in really good shape. I've maintained a slender figure all the way into my forties. But it wasn't always sunshine and rainbows. Again, having grown up in a dance environment, I was constantly told that I was fat. It was reinforced with every dirty look and every snide comment from my dance instructor. I was about 5 feet 8 and probably weighed about 115 or 120 pounds. And I was told I was fat. It was very disturbing and I'm surprised I didn't end up with an eating disorder. I will admit that throughout high school and college I took my share of diet pills. I see now the wisdom of exercise, not only to maintain weight health, but also as a stress reducer.

Once I moved to Santa Barbara I realized that my then-sedentary job would lead to problems and I should find something to do. I joined countless gyms apparently for the sheer luxury of paying to be a member and not going. Once I even faxed my cancellation to a gym that was right across the street rather than just going over. Pathetic. I did Curves for a while and really did enjoy it. I saw a few inches come off and a few percentage points come off my body fat. But I found reverse discrimination there. I had people calling attention to my slim figure, my flexibility when I stretched, and I was asked by numerous people why I was even there…I didn't need it. I found that offensive. It's not appropriate to say to a fat person, "Geez, good thing you're working out today, you're really fat." So why is it ok to say to me that I don't need to be there because I'm so thin. I finally left that club too and was feeling pretty lost.

My husband came home from jury duty one day and told me he had met a woman who did hip-hop. I wondered about hip-hop. I loved watching it but never tried it. He encouraged me to go to class. I looked it up online and a few weeks later found myself sitting in a parking lot scared to death to try to dance class again. I was talking to my dad on the cell phone as I waited for class and expressed my unease about stepping into a dance class after twenty years. He said, "Do the best you can;

you'll be fine." Encouraging as always. I showed up to the class and met the dance instructor, Tamarr Paul, who was amazingly energetic and somewhat intimidating. I made it through class without killing myself or hurting anyone around me. At one point he dragged me out of the back row saying, "You're kicking ass," and put me in the front of the room. Terrifying! I called my dad after class sweaty, out of breath and with a headache starting and told him I finished. And he said "And what, it took ten minutes for it to come back, didn't it?" Yes, it certainly did.

I realized after that class how much passion I had for dance. It strengthens not only my body but also my mind as I struggle to keep up with the next 5, 6, 7, 8. Tamarr's choreography was complicated, intricate and so filled with energy that there were times I could barely keep up. But I persisted. I went every Saturday for quite a few months. And then I realized that once a week was not enough. And how did I ever live without dance in my life? When looking through my old dance pictures I found one of me in a T-shirt that said, "To dance is to live." I remembered that it was. I decided that I was giving so much to my clients and very little to myself. So I reworked my schedule so that one or two nights a week I could go to do some more dance. Soon I was dancing five times a week. And I moved to the front row.

Kathy in hip hop

Tamarr announced that we were going to dance in the local Solstice Parade and I jumped at the opportunity to once again perform in front of a crowd. It was a long haul up State St. here in Santa Barbara but at the end I turned to the gal next to me and said, "Can we do it again?"

Solstice parade

She thought I was nuts. We did a few flash mobs, another stint in the Solstice Parade and I realized dance is still a complete and utter passion of mine. I let very few things interfere with my dance classes now. The reason I do it is that it keeps me young, it keeps me active, it keeps my brain working. It's allowed me to meet some amazing people, some I've been able to help. It's my drug, my church, my exercise. And never again will I let it fade from my life.

Find *your* dance, your trapeze, whatever makes you feel alive. And do it. Frequently. Exercise not only helps you maintain weight, but it also allows you to eat more of the things that you want to. I can choose to have the extra glass of wine or piece of bread because I know I've worked off those calories. Exercise boosts our metabolism, helps burn fat, helps with stress and keeps our minds sharp. Move your body in whatever way you find works best for you and enjoy!

Kathy at 22

Kathy at 42

SING THE BODY ELECTRIC: SOMATICIZING

⟲————⟲

S ometimes the words we use can unlock a mystery to what's happening in the body. This is what I discovered in my massage practice about the connection between the body and the mind.

I first discovered the power of the mind/body connection with a client who was having hand and wrist issues. I would do massage and her symptoms would disappear but within days they would return. I was frustrated that she seemed to be at an impasse with her healing. I knew she was doing her "homework" – stretching, ice, vitamins, taking breaks at work, adjusting her workstation – but nothing was helping to effect permanent change in her condition. I was getting irritated that I couldn't get her over that hump and I expressed my frustration to her. We started to discuss her pain and I asked again when it hurt the most. She said, "When I'm gripping things, grasping them. I have trouble holding my hairdryer and I can't lift my wine glass." I thought *that* was a tragedy so I figured we had to do something, and quickly. Her description ran through my head a few times and I concentrated on the words… grip, grasp…and I asked her, "Is there something you're holding too tightly? Is there something you need to let go?" Then I opened my hand.

She looked at me and her answer stunned me. Honestly, the fact that she had an answer at all stunned me. She very soulfully said, "I don't want to let my kids go." She went on to tell me how her brother was killed in a car crash right after he got his driver's license and how that broke the family apart and what it did to her parents. Her kids were now at that age, and she was terrified to give them the freedom she knew they needed. We discussed this a bit further during the rest of the massage; she made another appointment and left. In the time between appointments, she talked about her experience with her husband...and her kids. She told them the story that she had never shared before and was honest with them about her fear. When I saw her next, her pain had decreased and soon her treatments lasted longer until she no longer needed to see me. That fear, that need to let go, was the final step in her healing.

After my experience with that client, I started to pay more attention to the words and the phrases that clients chose to describe what was happening in their bodies. I also listened, in general, to how they spoke of their lives. Did they constantly speak negatively about their condition and their life? I had one client walk into my office, her very first appointment with me, and say, "My neck's been hurting forever, nothing helps, you probably can't do anything for me....should I take my clothes off?" I thought, "Well, you can give it a shot, but with that attitude, I'm not sure I can help you." During the sessions I tried to encourage her to change her verbiage. If she didn't believe she'd ever feel better, then how could she? I spent just as much time speaking with her about her language as I did her physical condition.

At that time, I was in a class for my master's degree where Louise Hay's book *Heal Your Life* was being used as a text. She was talking about self-love and how every day we should look in the mirror and say, "I love and accept myself just the way I am." This is a very effective tool for self-healing. I mentioned this to my negative client, thinking it could be really beneficial for her. She laughed and said, "Oh, I could never do that...I don't get that whole self-love thing. I mean, what does that even mean?" I was flabbergasted. She could NEVER do that? It struck me as sort of sad, that someone couldn't look in the mirror and say that they loved themselves. How can we not love ourselves?

I pointed out that she swam almost every day, she ate good food, she played bridge with her friends, she took the time to come see me. I asked if she enjoyed all those things. She answered affirmatively. Then I said, "That is self-love." She got it. I worked with her at great length to reflect on how she talked about her body. If someone asked how she was doing she either answered in the socially correct fashion of "Fine" or went on some long tirade about how horrible everything was. I believed that the more she belittled her body and told herself and everyone else how bad it was, it would only be too happy to oblige.

Over time she stopped referring to her neck as stupid, dumb and annoying and began to love every part of herself. She started doing affirmations while she swam, imaging her neck getting stronger with every arm stroke, and though I honestly can't say that it reduced her pain, it certainly gave her the ability to deal with it better. Sometimes just changing how we feel about something is healing enough. Positive thoughts can do wonders.

What was interesting about this particular client was how she got to this negative state. She gave birth to a child who was severely brain-damaged and he lived for eighteen years before he died. He was born in March and died in May. And every year from March to May she would get depressed. She would relive every painful memory, overwhelmed by feelings of guilt, anger, rage, and helplessness. She would welcome those feelings in. She practically scheduled them on the calendar. And though I will talk about how important it is to acknowledge and honor our emotions, reliving something that happened thirty years ago over and over again is not a healthy choice. When I first asked her what she was doing when her neck hurt her, she answered, "I can't turn my head to look back; it hurts." At that point I realized all she was doing was looking back.

To me, the mind is a vast computer and what we seek, we find. It's like typing keywords into your search engine of choice. If you're looking for information about massage, you type in massage; if you're looking for cats, you type in cats; if you want to read about Britney Spears, you don't type in the words Karl Malden. So, if we are programming our minds for sickness, illness, lack, poverty, suffering, fear and hatred, that is exactly what we are going to get. This is where affirmations can be useful. I discuss affirmations in depth on page 149.

The most important thing is to recognize situations where you tend toward negativity and decide to change your mind. No one can do this for you and often we're not ready to give up the thought process and change. It can be very scary and it's a lot of hard work. But going into situations with a negative attitude doesn't benefit anyone and just makes life unpleasant.

I've also observed, like the woman with the wrist issue, that the area of pain can indicate what is stuck emotionally. Here are a few examples:

-Hand and wrist: get a grip, grasping too tightly, feel like their hands are full

-Low back: support issues, feeling spineless, stabbed in the back, sexual issues

-Lower leg: moving forward, taking the next step

-Neck: Who's the pain in the neck?

-Sciatica: Who's the pain in the butt?

Here's a list I've put together of some of the phrases in this society that have body/mind connections. Do any of these sound familiar to you?

A big mouth
A chip on your shoulder
Big-hearted
Bleeding heart
Bone of contention
Broken-hearted
Can't get you out of my head
Can't put my finger on it
Can't stomach it
Cold-blooded
Cold feet
Cold shoulder
Cost an arm and a leg
Cross your mind
Doesn't have a leg to stand on
Elbow grease
Elbow your way in
Elbow room
From the bottom of your heart
Get a leg up
Getting on my nerves
Get off my back
Get under my skin
Give my right arm for...
Going out of my mind/head
Got your back
Grab the opportunity

Grasping at straws
Greet someone with open arms
Gut feeling (we've all felt this one, haven't we?)
Have no backbone
Have your back against the wall
Have heart
He has gall
He's soured to the experience (GERD?)
Heart of gold
Heart set on something
Heart-to-heart talk
Heartache
Heartbreak
Heartfelt
Heavy-hearted
I can't get a grip
I can't stomach this
I don't have the heart to do it
It's burning me up
It's eating at me (ulcer brewing?)
Jump in with both feet
Keep someone at arm's length
Know it like the back of your hand
Lend a hand
Longs for the sweetness (related to diabetes)
Lose heart
Lump in your throat
Makes me sick to my stomach
Makes my skin crawl
Mouthing off
Moving forward (lower legs)
My hands are full
My heart is blocked (clogged arteries/arteriosclerosis)
My heart is heavy
My stomach is in knots
No support (back issues)
Now I can breathe easy (feeling of relief; was there
    asthma or bronchitis before?)
Open heart

Open mind
Pain in the ass (piriformis and sciatic issues)
Pain in the neck
Point the finger at someone
Put my foot in my mouth
Put one foot in front of the other
Put your best foot forward
Rug is pulled out from under you
Save face
Sigh of relief
Shake a leg
Shoot from the hip
Shoulder the burden
Slipped out of my grasp
Someone to lean on
Spineless
Stabbed in the back (pain between the shoulder blades)
Stand on my own two feet
Start off on the wrong foot
Take something to heart
Takes your breath away
To be on your last leg
Tongue-tied
Turn a blind eye
Turn your back on someone
Up to his elbows
Wait on someone hand and foot
Walk the talk
Wears his heart on his sleeve
Weighing on me
Weight of the world is on my shoulders
Welcome someone with open arms
What are you gripping too tightly?
You're such a headache
You've got guts

I also encourage people to avoid saying that something is "killing" them. I don't think that's the best thing to be programming.

Noticing where you are suffering and thinking of these common phrases can help you get to the emotional root of what is causing the pain. Again, I'm not saying pain and illness is 100 percent emotional. Your back might hurt because you lifted incorrectly or your neck is sore because you cradle the phone against your shoulder. Even with that, it can't hurt to investigate the emotional components. There is a condition called **somatization disorder**, when there is no clear physical reason for the pain, but there seems to be an emotional link. Somatizers are people whose medical problems are a physical manifestation of emotional conflicts that stay unconscious. Like energy in physics, the stress caused by these conflicts cannot be destroyed, but is transformed into physical symptoms. The physical is a lot more easily dealt with than the emotional. Many people's physical symptoms get worse with stress, but the somatizer's pain is almost exclusively connected to the emotions. Tens of billions of dollars a year are spent on medical care for somatizers as they go from doctor to doctor to find out what's wrong.

Here is a personal example, not of somatizing, but of the connection between the thoughts and the physical.

Several years ago on a Monday morning, I went out to change the water in the birdbath, something I did every day. That particular day, I lifted the concrete bath and felt searing pain in my low back and heard a squishing noise. It dropped me to my knees *and* scared the daylights out of me. I was in so much pain I couldn't stand up, let alone replace the birdbath. I crawled into the house crying and called for my husband to get me some ice. I lay on the floor terrified. I remembered all the clients I had who had sustained back injuries and how they couldn't sit, stand, walk, work, drive, have sex, dance, move or function at all and I became very scared. My husband retrieved the ice and called the chiropractor and then asked me what happened. I didn't know. He told me to lie there and figure it out. (I love when he reminds me to do that.) So I did. I lay there thinking about the situation.

What was different about that day? Nothing. What was I doing another way? Nothing. What was I thinking about? *That* got my attention. At the moment I had done the lifting, I was thinking about my workweek. I had had a few clients who cancelled, which left some gaps in my schedule. For some reason, this time it made me fearful. Fearful that I didn't have enough, that I wouldn't make it, that I had failed. It was a visceral feeling in my gut even as I lay on ice and recounted it. I had to analyze those thoughts. Was it really failure? Did I truly not have enough? Were three clients cancelling actually going to cause my business to fail? Clearly, the answer to that was NO. But for some reason, at that moment, I was vulnerable to that fear.

As I had this realization, warmth spread through my back. I learned many years ago that low back problems are related to money issues, sex issues, and personal relationship and support issues. Wow! The money one hit me, big time. I did some self-talk about the situation, checked my bank account to confirm I wasn't going to be homeless in the next five days and told my body it had until Thursday to be better. (Programming recovery time actually does work.) I had massage, chiropractic, ice, ibuprofen and said positive affirmations about my life, my practice and my finances, and by Thursday I was fit as a fiddle. This back issue has recurred only two other times, both on Monday mornings and both when I was overly and irrationally concerned about money. Are there times we really have to be concerned about money? Heck, yeah! But this time it was fear and insecurity about the subject. It was unfounded, irrational fear. I looked at my bank account and could see that I would be okay with fewer clients that week. This simple observation gave me back control, not to mention a well-deserved rest. I wasn't a slave to my feelings anymore.

(Just a note. I've learned that if your body needs rest and you aren't giving it rest, it will *make* you rest, or give you a cold, an injury, and things getting cancelled. I don't recommend waiting for these things to give you a break; make the choice yourself.)

Now, what is the point of that story? I pinpointed the emotional cause of my issue and erased it, which I believe helped my healing. It illustrated in a very personal way that our emotions and thoughts can affect our bodies. And most important, that no matter how much work I do on this subject, I am vulnerable too!

If you notice that these things apply to you or a practitioner points it out, you might start thinking about other aspects of your life from this perspective. Self-examination, in an honest way, is the cornerstone of health. Sometimes we can't see these things in ourselves and we need a professional to help guide us.

Here's another example. A client came to me with neck pain. (Who is the pain in the neck?) During the course of the massage, he was telling me about his newly diagnosed ulcer and that there was burning and then stuff would bubble up. This sounded to me like unexpressed anger so I asked, "Is there something that's eating at you?" This is how the conversation continued.

Me: Ulcer, that sounds awful. Is there something that's eating at you?

Him: Well, the doctor said I have too much stomach acid.

Me: Yes, but is there something that is eating away at you?

Him: It seems to be spicy foods.

Me: Sure, but I mean, is there something that is eating at you and then bubbles up to the surface? (I said it more dramatically and with hand gestures this time.)

Him: (thinks for a second) Oh, I get it…I see what you're saying. Sure…tomatoes, peppers, garlic….

He wasn't ready to make the leap to connecting the mind and body. I suspected it was the relationship with his boss and, interestingly, as soon as he left his job, the ulcer started to clear.

Now, I'm not saying we should be running out to leave our jobs, our wives or husbands, etc. Sometimes we can't escape a stressful situation, but we can find ways to deal with it from a positive place. Focus on the positive, whether it's the view from the office, a coworker whom you like or just a paycheck. Focusing on the positive and not dwelling on the negative can sometimes make all the difference in the world. We have three choices in a stressful situation. Leave the situation, change the situation or change yourself.

I had a male client who was having horrible low back pain. His job involved lots of climbing around on the floor in uncomfortable positions and heavy lifting. This pain was impacting his ability to do his job. About halfway through the massage, after acknowledging that this certainly could be a profession-related issue and that there was a leg length difference *and* that his piriformis (attaches to the sacrum and top of the femur) and quadratus lumborum (muscles in the low back) certainly were tight,

I asked if he found a connection between the level of pain and his stress level. He said there was.

I then mentioned to him that the low back often represented money and personal support issues. He was quiet for a very long time and I wondered if he was pondering, ignoring me or had simply fallen asleep. About twenty minutes went by before he gave me the following response: "Yeah, interesting. I've been pretty stressed about money. My business is pretty slow right now. I'm still working, but I'm afraid of what might happen if I don't get some new clients in." I think it was the first time he vocalized that fear out loud. He then mentioned that he was also afraid to tell his wife. He let out a big sigh and I felt his body relax a few degrees. He didn't want to be seen as a failure or make her worry. I suggested that perhaps sharing that with her might decrease the stress he was feeling. Perhaps they could meet the issue head on and she could support him emotionally through the fear that he was feeling. He agreed.

The next time I saw him, there had been some improvement in his pain level. His muscles were less tight and in general, he seemed happier. He had shared his concerns with his wife over dinner that previous week and they had a great conversation about finances and his job. After putting pen to paper and working some things out, they realized that even if he never got busier, they would still be perfectly fine, and it brought them closer.

I could have just massaged him and helped his back from the physical aspect, but by asking a few questions, he was able to find deeper healing. It can be that simple. We might just have to ask the body what the pain is trying to tell us and then listen for the answer.

People have asked me why everyone doesn't have low back pain then, since the issues connected to it are universal. And that is a very valid question. What I've observed is that the pain often manifests when it is a long-term, unacknowledged emotional issue, a habitual thought or something very threatening and acute like my sudden money fear. Once we process the emotion and start to feel in control, the pain and the emotional pattern ends. You will most likely still need to do the physical things like massage, chiropractic, ice, etc. Clearing the emotional pattern can also bring healing and we'll explore numerous techniques to do just that.

Remember that for true health, we need to balance all aspects of body, mind and spirit. And perhaps some of our physical manifestations of illness have an emotional trigger. Affirmations can help, as can analyzing what situations we treat from a negative mindset. Our words and thoughts have a larger influence on our physicality than we realize. If we can integrate the emotions with the physical, perhaps we can achieve full and long-lasting healing.

Once we pay attention to the connection of the mind/body in one area, it spills over to other areas of our lives as well. I bet when my client experiences future illnesses, he might also examine those from a mind/body perspective. Doing so can help heal all aspects of life.

Speaking of healing, let's talk about healing vs. curing. Now, according to my license and the FDA/AMA, I'm not allowed to be curing. That word alone can get me in big trouble, but I'm going to use it here for my purposes. (Don't tell.) The word *cure* comes from the root meaning "care, concern and attention." The word *heal* comes from the root meaning "to make whole." The curing often comes from an external source: a pill, surgery, intervention or procedure. The healing comes from within. It is absolutely possible that the two can exist exclusive of one another. Here's another example.

Another client came in with neck pain. Again, I wondered who was the pain in his neck. We discussed this briefly and I asked what else was happening with his body. He told me that he had blood in his urine. WAY beyond my scope of practice as a massage therapist. I asked the requisite questions. Have you seen your doctor? Is there any pain? Are you having any other symptoms? And he assured me that he was seeing his doctor in two days and he was probably just passing a kidney stone, he gets them all the time. (Ow!) I looked up some stuff in my symptom handbook, we talked for another second and I got him on the table. As I worked on his neck we had the following conversation:

Me: So, blood in the urine huh?

Him: Yeah.

Me: So, anything you might be pissed off about?

Him: Oh…yeah, I get it…blood in the urine, pissed, yeah, I get it.

Me: So?

Him: Nope, nothing I'm pissed about. But I get it.

Me: Oh, ok, because I know you're frustrated with your job and would like things to be different there, so I didn't know if it escalated to pissed off.

Him: No, not pissed off.

Me: Ok

So I dropped it. And we were quiet for about three minutes until he started talking about his job. He told me how no one does their work and everyone is stupid and he couldn't wait to retire, but has three more years before his full pension, and why can't anyone do what they're supposed to? He wished he could leave now, but just can't and what is wrong with people. I'm thinking, "Hmmm, he sounds kinda pissed off," but I just let him keep talking and he ended the tirade with, "But I'm not pissed off, I'm not pissed off...there's just this...this...series of little irritations."

I said, "Oh, like kidney stones?" He laughed uncomfortably and sadly said, "Yeah." And the conversation ended.

Well, it turned out that he didn't have kidney stones; he had bladder cancer. And he did the smartest thing he could have done. He quit his job. Three years early, with a lower pension and not as good health insurance. I fully believe had he not quit, his cancer would have come back. And I also believe that, had this been addressed more fully when it was just kidney stones, it might not have escalated to cancer. He went through the curing which the doctors provided, but he also went through the healing, which he did himself. To this day he remains cancer free.

See, here's the thing about the mind and emotions. They don't like to be ignored or stuffed or diminished. If we don't acknowledge them, they will have a tantrum like a child in the supermarket. It starts out with "Mommy, Mommy, Mommy," and tugging on the skirt and soon, if ignored long enough, they will start ripping things off shelves. His kidney stones were "Mommy, Mommy" and the cancer was the tantrum. Now, again, there are numerous causes for disease and please don't misunderstand: By no means am I saying that he *caused* his own cancer. I'm saying the stuffed emotions contributed. I am pointing out an observation: *illness picks the area of vulnerability and expresses things that are previously unexpressed, typically after a bout of stress.* If we can't find a way to deal with our reactions to stress, it gives the same result. And as you can tell, I do a lot of talking about stress and ways of dealing with it.

MODELING

As I mentioned before, because I grew up dancing I was always extraordinarily body-conscious. I have a very thin waist and very round hips so if I bought clothes to fit my hips, they would sag in the waist and if I bought them to fit my waist, I couldn't get them up over my hips. For those people who have truly struggled with weight, I know this sounds like a horrible problem, right? I'm being sarcastic. I totally understand and sympathize with those people who truly have weight issues. But to me, mine was a big deal. I was living in Los Angeles and a photographer friend called me and said he needed a model for his art class. And would I be interested? It paid $35 for three hours. That sounded great to me. I asked what I should wear. He paused for a minute and then said, "No, no. It's nude." I pondered for just a moment. Could I really stand in a room full of strangers naked while they sketched me? I decided I could. And I thought it would be an interesting experience.

I showed up at his studio in Los Angeles and there were about ten people in the room. He introduced me to them and then told me to put my robe on. What robe? Who the hell had a robe? I was a complete newbie at this and I could see the people were amused at my lack of knowledge of the subject. Luckily he had one and I changed in the other room. He set up some lighting, I came out onto the model stand and he said, "Okay." And I just looked at him. "Okay what?" "Pose," he said. I had no idea what I was doing. I dropped the robe and did the first thing I thought of which was a ballet position. Seemed like a simple thing to hold for five minutes. But let me tell you, nothing is simple to hold for five minutes. Let alone when you get into the longer poses. After the first few quick sketches, I found my creative juices were flowing. I could tell where the light was going to hit me and how the angles were going to look for the people drawing me. At one point I did a reclining pose on my side, the curve of my hip and my waist facing a light.

We were going to take a break so I put on my robe and asked if I could walk around and look at the drawings. I was very curious to see how I looked to the artists. I walked over to one woman's in particular. It was a beautiful drawing filled with life with smooth curved lines, an absolute beauty flowing from within. She asked if she could show me her favorite part of the drawing. "Of course," I said. She pointed to the part where my round hips met my small waist and she said, "Look at that beautiful curve. It's like the mountains meeting the sea. This is truly art. It's just spectacular." I stepped back and looked at it. It was beautiful. I had a new appreciation for my body and as I walked around and looked at all the other artists, I began to see through their eyes. I began to look at my body as perfection, as a piece of art. No matter where the lumps were, if you could see the cellulite, where things squished together, what I saw there was beauty in all of that. And this room full of artists taught me that our bodies are divine in their art.

After that class I could never again feel self-conscious in clothes or a bathing suit. *People had told me my body was art.* I have carried that with me since. And I've had the privilege of modeling for hundreds of artists. A few of the drawings and paintings hang in my own home. I recommend that everybody model for an art class. If you're not comfortable with nudity or don't want to do that for religious reasons, put on a bathing suit or underwear. Pose for someone. Look at the art in your body and see you for what you truly are. Which is a work of perfection.

DÉJÀ VU ALL OVER AGAIN: CANCER

Since I started this whole book talking about my mother dying from cancer, I figured I should probably address cancer itself. Since my mother's death in 1988, I have lost countless friends, family and clients to cancer. A few have stood out. I'll tell you some of their stories and then share a few of my tips for cancer.

One woman came to me already terminal. I don't know how she found me but she was in pretty bad shape. Now, looking back and even then I suspected she had some level of mental illness. She was 49 years old and her mother dropped her off. She left her in my parking lot with them screaming at each other as the car lurched away. As this new client walked toward me she shuffled, she had very little hair after chemotherapy, she was skinny, she looked just like my mom before she died. I didn't know if I could handle it. She introduced herself and I asked what I could do for her. She told me that she was terminal, had tumors throughout her body and there probably wasn't much I could do. In essence she had no idea why she was there. Throughout the weeks leading up to her death, I saw her at least once or twice a week.

When she could no longer drive or hitch a ride from a friend, I would leave my office, drive to her house, pick her up and drive her back to my office, do the treatment and drive her back to her house. I never officially charged her; she paid me what she could. Some days I would do Reiki on her. Some days I would rub her hands and feet. Some days I would just hold her and other days I would leave the room and she would scream and cry in my office. After my first appointment with her, I was emotionally raw the rest of the day. It was so much like my mom. I got home that night at dinner and was telling my husband. As I was describing her and relating her to my mother, I started to tear up and I turned to my husband and said, "I'm not sure I can do this." He looked at me and took my hand and said, "You have to. For you and for her." So I did.

A few weeks into our session she finally admitted to me that she knew she was dying, but wanted to keep it a secret from her daughter. I was now in a very tough spot as I could relate to both being the adult and the child. There were times I found that time confused me and I could put myself so clearly back inside an eighteen-year-old kid dealing with her mother dying. Her daughter was twenty and away at college. She made me promise that if she died I would not let her daughter know. I denied that request and said, "She's already going to be heartbroken. Do you want her to be pissed off too?" I was actually stunned that her daughter didn't know she was dying. It was so apparent that she had so little time left.

When I had the privilege of meeting the daughter, she and I talked about that. I said, "What if you find out your mother is going to die?" She said, "I don't believe she is. Perhaps it should be apparent to me but you just don't expect that to happen so I can't see it." I remembered that I too was in a position where I had no idea my mother was dying. I assumed she would be in and out of the hospital as normal and would come home and get better. It was never explained to me that she was dying. I wish it had been. I think parents and adults underestimate the ability of children, whether eight or eighteen, to deal with such news.

Luckily she withheld her death until her daughter returned. She was finally taken out of her little cluttered apartment and put into hospice care in the hospital. I sat with her the day before she died and held her hand. She was unconscious and heavily on morphine. I told her it was okay to go whenever she wanted to. Her breath quickened and I could tell she was panicking. I told her we all loved her and that she could take her time. She calmed. I left and again showed up the next day. I sat by her side and told her we loved her and that she could go whenever she wanted. Her breathing slowed, she let out a sigh and twenty minutes later she was gone. I had just gone back to my office so I missed that moment of transition, but her mother and daughter were at her side.

My relationship with her was a very versatile one, as I was acting more as counselor and friend, not just her massage therapist. I tried to be whatever she needed in the moment. She was very isolated and did not connect to many people. She had very little sense of humor and at times I would make a joke and she would just look at me. The day I actually got her to heartily laugh I knew I had won. She called me one day and left a message to simply say, "I love you." I will cherish that message so long as I live. About six weeks after her death I reached out to her daughter. I remembered how alone and confused I was when my mother died with no one around to guide me. I asked if I could do anything for her and we talked and laughed briefly and we hung up the phone. I knew that would be my last conversation with her as I was not there for her but for her mother. I still cherish this woman deep in my heart and hope her family is well. Though there was no cure for this frail woman, there was healing. And I like to think I helped bring just a bit to her.

Another one of my clients who passed away more recently was a hero of mine. She had survived breast cancer over twenty years ago and then found herself rediagnosed with esophageal cancer. She lasted quite a long period of time, having gone through chemo and radiation. But by that point they had over-radiated her and surgery was not an option. I watched her get less and less energetic and wither away with weight loss and more pain. At times you could see the tumor bulging out of her throat. I can't imagine the pain that she was enduring. I knew her before her cancer diagnosis. She would come to me occasionally for stress reduction and I learned that she was just as Type A as I was. She was driven and powerful, a courageous woman. After her cancer I would see her weekly. Sometimes I would do Reiki and visualization. Sometimes I would massage her hands or feet or whole body. She loved angels and was an angel herself. I would do Reiki on her and we would visualize angels swooping in to take away the tumors. She started to feel better. She started to exercise again. But her next scan showed that not only were the tumors not shrinking, they were actually getting bigger. I kind of wish they wouldn't have told her that because as soon as she learned that news, she stopped exercising and the dinner parties ceased. She died soon after that.

During her visualizations she said it was the only time she felt in control. She felt that people were just doing things *to* her and making decisions *about* her and that she had no choices. She was put in a beautiful hospice environment. And on the day of what I figured would be my last massage with her, I didn't get to see her, as she passed moments before I left my office to go. Another great loss of humanity. But she went surrounded by friends and family with much love.

I've dealt recently with clients as young as thirty. One dealt with mesothelioma and another, colon cancer; this young man lost his rectum during treatment and at his young age is relegated to a colostomy bag. And they weren't sure they got all the cancer, he seems to be riddled with it. So many sad stories and lost lives.

Not all my cancer stories end with tragedy. I've had a few clients who surprisingly had to have lumps removed, or go through radiation or chemo. But one client has definitely become a hero. He has survived so much and his journey with medical treatments isn't quite over yet. It was discovered that he had esophageal cancer. He went through chemo and radiation and we thought the cancer was gone. But his next scan showed it had returned and was growing quickly. They rushed him into surgery where they took out half of his jaw and replaced it with his own shinbone. To look at him now, you would have no idea that his face was not his own.

He has been dealing with pain, discomfort, the inability to swallow and has been eating through a feeding tube for months and months. I helped him with his rehab in loosening up his throat and jaw and getting him to swallow. Unfortunately the doctor sent him to a lymphic drainage therapist and in reality the problem wasn't lymph, it was scar tissue. I believe had they caught that earlier, we could have had better results. I see him twice a week and his courage has amazed me. There have been a very few times where he's broken down or seemed to be in a bad mood. He is certainly a survivor. I see him to this day. He has had continued trouble with his feeding tube and the newest frustration is that they put a new kind in but didn't tell him how to use it. I sat down with an anatomy book and showed him exactly what was going on. He was relieved that I helped but furious that no one had given him the care that I did. It is truly an honor to deal with him and all of my clients whether suffering with cancer or not. Every person who lies on my table is a joy to be with and an education for me in life, healing and humanity. (A sad addendum to this chapter: as I was editing this book, my client with the throat cancer passed. I found out at three a.m. in a hotel room in Jordan. My sadness was inexplicable. I saw him the day before I left and I knew. I knew that it was the last time. I said very firmly, "Take care of yourself." And he just looked at me. I think he knew as well. Another giant cancer hole pierced my heart as I lost another special person in my life.)

What follows is a handout I put together on cancer. It's information gathered from multiple sources.

Cancer is the uncontrolled replication of cells. This happens in our bodies all the time and the immune system deals with the problem. When cancer takes hold and forms a tumor, we must boost the immune system to help fight it. Here are some suggestions.

Increase vitamin C. I mean craploads of it. Literally. Bowel tolerance is a way to tell when the body is done accepting it. If you spread the doses throughout the day, it's more easily tolerated and absorbed. Too much causes diarrhea, so you don't want to quite get to that point. If it happens, back off the dose.

Most cancer cannot live in oxygen or an alkalized environment. Deep breathing is beneficial, as is a hyperbaric chamber if you can find one. Liquid oxygen is available from health food stores to drip into water. As far as alkaline goes, there are supplements that work, also water systems that alkalize the drinking water, though I don't believe in drinking alkaline water all the time.

I suggest supplementing with pancreatic and/or digestive enzymes, depending on what organs are affected. Common digestive enzymes are protease, lipase and amylase. These are easily found in pill form. Also, a product called Wo-Benzymes has shown great effect in decreasing tumor size and boosting the immune system. (Multiple sources recommend this for cancer.)

Studies have shown how important attitude is with cancer outcome. *A fighting spirit wins.* This is the biggest competition you will ever be in, and fighting and staying positive will work wonders. Surround yourself with people who love you and *tell them to remain positive when around you.* Prayer is very powerful and people in a group thinking the same healing thoughts can be very beneficial.

Eliminating anything processed is recommended. Chemicals and preservatives in food just give your body something else to deal with. Whole foods, fruits and vegetables are key. I personally would avoid wheat and dairy, as they can be hard on the system. Keeping up the nutrition is very important and a good multivitamin/mineral and amino acid formula would be valuable. Some experts recommend a macrobiotic diet, or at the very least going organic, vegetarian. If you can handle the restrictions, it's not a bad idea, but make sure you get enough protein and amino acids.

In my schooling on cancer treatment, we learned about the Hoxsey Center in Mexico. I studied this man Harry Hoxsey and his center in Tijuana at great length. Though he passed away several years ago, his clinic is going strong and shows a great success rate with cancer. http://www.hoxseybiomedical.com/clinic-information/

A recent article on soothing the pain of chemotherapy recommended 1000mg Green Tea Extract, 20mg melatonin (at bedtime for sleep) and a multivitamin with at least 1000mg of Vitamin C.

Zinc is a great supplement for boosting the immune system. 150mg/day helped reduce the effects of radiation therapy also.

Another source recommends melatonin at night, saying it increased survival and improved quality of life.

N-acetylcysteine (NAC) decreased the negative effects of chemotherapy agents. They recommend 1000mg, given 90 minutes before chemo treatment.

When I was learning about Dr. Hoxsey, another treatment was mentioned. This is from another man who was consistently persecuted for curing cancer in America. He had a formula called Essiac, which is still available. www.essiac-canada.com I had a client who used this on her husband with melanoma and his recovery was much quicker.

From *Prescription for Nutritional Healing*:

Nutrients that are recommended:

Coenzyme Q10
Garlic
Melatonin, again
Omega 3 fatty acids (fish oil)
Wobenzymes, again
Shark Cartilage
Superoxide Dismutase (can be injected by doctor)
Vitamins A and E, B and C

Recommended as important:

Maitake and shiitake/reishi mushrooms to boost immune system and they have anti-tumor properties

Helpful:

Acidophilus: helps promote good bacteria in the colon
Grape seed extract, a powerful antioxidant
Multivitamin and mineral

From *Prescription for Herbal Healing*:
Drinking licorice tea can help with nausea during chemo,

During chemotherapy, greet it as a positive thing. As it's going into your body, picture it fighting that cancer, see the tumors shrinking. If you fight against the chemo and dread it, it will not work as well for you.

Dr. Donald Abrams recommends in one of his videos that people undergoing chemo should take the following compounds.

(Please remember what I said in the chapter on herbs: these are chemicals and can interact with drugs and each other. Check with a qualified practitioner or your doctor before taking any of these. And I'm not a doctor, I just pass on info. Do your own research and ask questions.)

Vitamin D3 (in a liquid or gel tab)

Calcium/Magnesium

Omega 3 fatty acids (not Omega 6) – use liquid or gel beads and refrigerate. Use Omega 3 eggs. We need a balance of 3 and 6 but our food sources now have too much Omega 6 – some 20 times more than in the 1950s. Does not recommend Cod Liver Oil, as it may have too much Vitamin A.

Medicinal Mushrooms – (Non-specific immune stimulants - Don't cure cancer but are good adjuncts to chemotherapy. All mushrooms need to be **cooked**!)

Coriolus - Turkey tail – aka Yun Zhi - "not edible" so use capsules: ±25% of cancer costs in Japan devoted to use of this – PSK and PSP formulations - particularly use for gastro-intestinal and breast cancer.

Shiitake – better to eat the whole food (cooked).

Maitake – may decrease chemo therapy side effects (cooked).

Reishi (the mushroom of immortality) – may inhibit tumor cell growth – recommends a tincture or capsule.

Cordyceps – (used by Chinese in Olympics) highly oxygenated – normally found in Tibet but now cloned for production... lung & kidney tonic – may improve anemia and side effects of chemotherapy – very useful.

Lion's Mane – hericium – seems to promote nerve growth – peripheral neuropathy – during and after chemo – edible and delicious.

White Button, Crimini and Portobello mushrooms (cooked) – Very useful – particularly in breast cancer (especially when used with green tea).

Melatonin – at night – lowers breast cancer risk, good for brain and lung cancer

Coenzyme Q-10 – take as a gel bead (especially good for Herceptin).

Turmeric (curcumin & piperine together).

Glutamine, alpha linoleic, and Vitamin E – good for neuropathy.

Black Raspberry has good cancer risk-reducing effects – especially for gastrointestinal cancer.

Green tea – 4 or 5 cups a day (but not the extract – can damage the liver).

Be careful of **Vitamin A** – not recommended, especially for people with a history of smoking.

Does not recommend a lot of **Vitamin C** during chemotherapy (unless undergoing surgery).

Milk Thistle not during chemo – a liver protectant – protects against toxic chemicals – and might not be the best thing as it may interfere during chemo....

There are some great videos from UCSF Osher Center for Integrative Medicine about cancer and nutrition and health in general. Dr Abrams has some great resources there. I'm a fan! And please remember in reading all of what I have just written, that I am NOT a medical doctor and you should check with your practitioners before starting or stopping any new treatment.

A visualization/meditation for cancer:

Get into a relaxed place, in a comfortable position. Breathe deeply and try to quiet the mind. Get a picture in your head of what you think the cancer looks like. It can be a ball, a blob, whatever it is to you. See it on the organs. As you inhale, send the breath to that organ and tumor and picture it shooting at it, eating it, dissolving it, whatever scene works for you. I always saw it as the cavalry coming over the hill in the old movies to save the day. That cavalry is your white blood cells and they are surrounding the tumor to get rid of it. Hold the picture of the tumor disappearing for as long as you can. Do this visualization as many times during the day as you can. I've seen amazing things happen with this type of visualization.

SURGERY SOLUTIONS:
WHAT A CUT-UP

———

In 1998 I turned to place an order at a drive-through window and I realized I didn't have a voice. Not in the esoteric sense of having a voice, I seriously couldn't speak. If I turned my head to the left my voice went away. This was disconcerting to me, to say the least, and when I got home to enjoy my Burger King hamburger, I looked in the mirror and saw a very large lump. I had not noticed it before. I do remember a few days previously I was getting a massage. I was facedown on the table and the practitioner was pushing down on my neck and my throat was hitting the bar. It was uncomfortable but I couldn't find my voice to say stop. We see where this is going.

Throughout my life I didn't speak my mind or my truth. I had read Louise Hay's book that talked about things incorporating from an emotional state into the body. But imagine my shock and surprise when I looked in the mirror and actually saw a giant lump in my throat. I didn't have health insurance at that point in my life but I scurried off immediately to my doctor who looked at it, did an ultrasound and said, "You have cancer that has to come out immediately, I'll see you next week." I knew it wasn't cancer. Somewhere deep in my soul I knew it was not cancer. It wasn't denial of "no-no no." I was sure it wasn't cancer. It was truly a knowing. He left the room and I grabbed the lab results. I took them with me, because I didn't believe him. The way they read to me said there was no cancer. The way they read to him, there was cancer. I explained to him that I didn't have health insurance, he said they were sure they could work something out. I told him I didn't want a giant scar across my neck because I was an actress. He said that wasn't a problem and that they would cut into the wrinkles of my neck. I looked at him. I was twenty-five years old. "What wrinkles?" I questioned. He looked at me and said, "Well, where the wrinkles will be someday." Idiot.

Though I was sure this wasn't cancer, it really did scare me. To be so young and be facing what seemed to me to be a life-altering surgery. Hormones the rest of my life, giant scar on my throat. What if I had other complications or side effects? Would I die? I opted not only to not have the surgery, but to pretend the whole incident didn't exist. With the state of health insurance at that time, no one would take me with that diagnosis. So I erased all of that from my reality. The next time I applied for health insurance, it didn't exist. I never wrote it down.

But in my quest to avoid surgery, I tried everything. Homeopathy, Ayurvedic medicine, acupuncture and Chinese herbs, Reiki, past life regression, even poking at it and telling it to go away. That didn't work, by the way. I didn't think to use my construction worker (more on that in the chapter on visualization), but I did visualize ice melting, ants carrying it away. Nothing worked. Me, Miss Natural Health, and I didn't know how this was going to go away. It was growing at a rapid pace, larger and larger. It was overtaking my throat and I found I was having trouble swallowing. Though my voice did come back, it wasn't as strong as it was before the lump and some nights lying in bed when I swallowed I could hear the glump glump in my own ears. It was driving me crazy. And you could see it coming out of my neck, a giant lump.

With my new doctors and insurance, it had been tested multiple times and was **not, I repeat, not cancer.** No one ever suspected it was cancer other than the first doctor, who apparently had a boat payment to make. In 2008, my doctor was encouraging me to finally have this thing taken out. "It's got its own ZIP code, Kathy. Seriously, when are you gonna deal with this?" My hormones were perfect; I didn't want to take out a perfectly functioning thyroid. However, that year my husband lost his health insurance. I had gotten on his because it was so much cheaper than my individual plan. Big mistake. Because when I lost his, no one would take me with a diagnosis of a goiter. Goiter. And I couldn't get health insurance. I was young and healthy, I had no other problems but I could not get insurance because I had a benign lump in my throat that I swore I was never going to have removed. This was the year President Obama had decided to help everybody with their Cobra insurance. I was able to keep the plan I had for a mere $60 a month for six months. Guess who scheduled her surgery? I met with the surgeon, he assured me it would be quick and easy and, because it wasn't cancer, he could be not sloppy, exactly, but he didn't have to be as precise about getting every single cell of the thyroid. I scheduled my surgery. December 12. The same day many years previously I had left my home in Pittsburgh and started the drive across country to California. A pivotal date in my life, apparently.

I remembered when I had had my knee surgery a few years previously that I was privileged enough to use a really cool hypnotherapy tape series. It's called the Surgery Support Series and it's made by Hemi-Sync. Hemi-Sync is really innovative and phenomenal. It uses sound waves that activate both hemispheres of the brain and also give you hypnotic suggestions. There is one you listen to before the surgery, one during the surgery and one in recovery. Their series is amazing. And I'll talk more about my knee surgery in a minute. But let's stick with the thyroid. I borrowed those tapes, I started my homeopathic Arnica and I asked if my mother-in-law could be there. I really wanted a mom there. I prepped myself for the surgery using meditation, visualization and affirmations that I would heal quickly. After all these years of wondering how I would get my goiter to go away, I finally had my answer. Dr. Dunn would take it out. On some level I found it to be sort of a failure, but ultimately found it to be very empowering, as I was able to bring the best of both worlds together, the Western and complementary alternative medicine. My surgery went without a hitch and it was once again an illustration of how we can use all of the tools in our toolbox to make things work. I've had no issues with my neck or the hormones. I have fabulous doctors and they make all the difference. After my surgery I met with my endocrinologist, who is amazing, and we were talking about my hormones. I put my hands on my hips and said, "Dan, you better get these hormones right because I have boundless energy and don't gain weight. If I get tired and fat, I'm coming after you." He put his hands on his hips and said, "Kathy, my hormones are going to be perfect. If you get fat, you ate too much and it's your fault." And then we both laughed. I cannot stress enough how important your relationships are with your doctors and practitioners.

To me, the greatest illustration of what I was able to do with surgery was my knee and my toe. Let's start with the knee first. It was my first surgery ever and after several rounds of chiropractic and massage, I realized my torn meniscus was not going to be repaired. I finally asked my chiropractor, "Is there anything I can do to fix this other than surgery?" He said, "Nope." That was the final answer I needed. I scheduled my surgery in 2004 and it was one of the best things I ever did. I loved my surgeon, as he was not particularly anxious to operate until I was ready. I visualized, I did my affirmations, used my surgery tapes, took my BF and C (Bone, Flesh and Cartilage formula), my homeopathic Arnica. I prepped with chiropractic and massage, also including acupuncture. I was growing comfrey, also known as bone knit, in my garden and was ready to use that as well.

I recovered incredibly fast from the surgery. I had the surgery on a Thursday. I took Friday off. Saturday my husband and I went down to our outlet malls where I walked around and tried on clothes for a good two or three hours. We met a friend for lunch and then we walked around to shop for furniture. I still had a very large wrap on my knee and had many people questioning. When I told them I had just had surgery and they found out it was only two days previously, many of them said, "Why are you walking around?" Or questioned, "My God, woman, why aren't you in bed?" My response to that is, because I didn't want to be. I was not into getting attention through my pain or suffering. I expected to come out of the surgery feeling great and very mobile. And that is exactly what I manifested.

So much of our recovery depends on our expectations. It also helped that I did my preparation. We need to be active participants in our healing and cannot just rely on other people to do the work. The day after my surgery, I was at the chiropractic office for an adjustment. I visualized my construction worker getting to work on the knee and did my stretches, ice and comfrey. The only negative that came out of it is that I gave myself frostbite. Pretty funny, since I was in Southern California. At the time of this writing in 2015, I have had no further problems with my knee. The small meniscus surgery seems to have done the trick. And just a few months after the surgery I ran my first 5K. It was the worst two hours of my life. (Kidding.)

My most recent surgery, in 2014, was my toe. I had a large bone spur in the joint of my big toe. It came from an injury I had when I was about twenty. I had dropped a large can of pasta sauce right on the joint of my toe and some twenty years later, it was wreaking havoc. I was in pain when I danced, pain when I walked, pain when I ran, and was very uncomfortable in my favorite high heels. That combination of things propelled me into getting surgery. I asked one of my orthopedic friends to recommend someone. I chose another orthopedic surgeon as opposed to a podiatrist. He was a former engineer and totally resonated with me. When I finally decided I couldn't take the pain anymore, as it was hurting with everything I did, and since I wasn't about to give up dance, I scheduled my surgery.

In the weeks leading up to my surgery, I did hypnosis to turn off the pain. I could literally put two of my fingers together and say "Cancel" and the pain would go away. One of the reasons I think this works is that I knew the cause of the pain and I knew I was going to be dealing with it soon. I prepared my body with meditation, the BF and C, herbs, homeopathics and acupuncture. I made sure my body and mind were as prepared as possible for the surgery. The night before the surgery, I prepared myself with massage and listened to my pre-op tape, which basically was a progressive muscle relaxation. It's the Hemi-Sync tape series I had listened to for my other surgeries. During the massage my therapist did a lot of calf and foot work to make sure my body was as balanced as possible. I also had a chiropractic adjustment that day.

The morning of my surgery I made sure I was in a balanced state of mind. I did self-hypnosis and my meditation. I went into the surgery feeling positive and excited about the outcome. I knew it would work for me. As I lay in my little curtained cubicle waiting for my surgery, I listened to what was happening around me. The woman next to me had nothing to say but negative things. She expressed anger and frustration at everything and anyone who tried to help her. I decided at that point I certainly did not want to be that person, and she was probably more apt to have a negative outcome than I was. I see no need, no reason to be negative in these situations. The more you get yourself worked up and get combative to the people around you, the worse outcome you are going to have. I was joking with the nurses and the anesthesiologist and put myself in the most positive state possible.

Given my skill at self-hypnosis, I told the anesthesiologist that I did not want to be fully out. I would have preferred a local but they would not let me do that. He opted for twilight and put me completely out while they applied the local anesthesia and the tourniquet. I was moved into the surgery room, hoisted myself on the surgery table, pressed Play on my tape and I was gone. About halfway through the surgery, I awoke. I could feel tugging and banging on my toe. It was fascinating to me and I was hoping to be able to experience the sensation. I must have made a face because the next thing you know, I was out again. I awoke to my recovery tape telling me to be wide awake. I felt great.

My doctor, before the surgery, explained to me that I would have to be in a special shoe for four to six weeks. I said, "Oh, okay, so two." He looked at me puzzled, as if I didn't hear what he said, and said, "No, four to six." I said, "I heard you. I will be out of it in two." (I was actually out of it and in my real shoes in less than two and back in high heels in about three.) I was also given some pain pills. I was stunned that he was so adamant about my having to pick up the prescription for pain meds. I told him I would probably not need them but he encouraged me. When I picked up the prescription, I found 60 pills. Yes, 60. For a person who gets things from inference, what is that saying? It's saying, "Holy crap, you're going to be in a lot of pain." Luckily I do not work on inference. Before the surgery he asked if I had picked up my pain meds. I told him yes but I still wouldn't need them and was it really that painful. He said yes, most people are in tremendous amounts of pain, again programming me to need them. I understand the urgency to make sure I was protected. But what I think doctors have to understand is the enormous power they have over the patients. I have a very strong will and I'm not very suggestible to doctors. But most people are. And what he said to me would make anyone assume they were going to be in a tremendous amount of pain and our bodies are only too willing to follow suit. In the end, after the surgery I needed no pain pills. I took a few Advil over the first few days, but definitely did not need Vicodin as it was prescribed. They sit in the closet in case of some horrible accident.

I used my comfrey, my acupuncture needles, my homeopathics and my Arnica cream. When I saw him a mere five days after the surgery, he pulled off the bandages and said it looked like it had been weeks and not days. And that I was the exception, not the rule. What's fascinating is that I had a client having the exact same surgery the following week. She followed my protocol. She was also ahead of the game and was also told at her first visit that she was the exception, not the rule. I'm thinking, if the two of us can do it, any one of us can be the exception and why not make us the rule?

We don't give ourselves enough credit for the enormous power of our bodies to heal itself. And of our minds to participate. If I can do it and my client can do it and hundreds of thousands and maybe millions of other people have done it, you can do it too. Now, I'm not saying we should completely eschew Western medicine. I don't believe we can just sit around visualizing and heal everything in our bodies, though I wish that were true. What I am saying is, we have to combine the best of all worlds.

What follows is a very specific list of everything that I have done for my surgeries. Take what you will of these and leave the rest. But I do encourage you to try as many complementary things as you can to make your surgery experience more pleasant, especially if it is a surgery that is not elective. Having surgery for things like cancer or heart disease can be incredibly scary. Anything you can do to relax yourself before the procedure is going to empower you to heal quicker and more fully.

Not that elective surgery is any less nerve-racking, but at least you can have the peace of mind that you are voluntarily going into the surgery. And oftentimes you pick the date so you have more time and opportunity to put these things into practice. Here is my list.

– Pre-op:

Hypnosis and self-hypnosis to stop the pain, prepare for surgery, decrease stress

Stop smoking, have the best diet possible, lose weight if you need to and have the time. Even a few pounds will help

Start the homeopathic Arnica orally

Visualization to prep body for surgery

Pre-op CD from Hemi-Sync: http://shop.hemi-sync.com

– Intra-op (during surgery)

My journey:
Listened to the intra-op surgery tape
Meditated the morning of the surgery and did breathing and visualization during the moments leading up to the surgery. Listened to the post-op tape in recovery. (Give the tape/CD to the nurse in advance with instructions to change the tapes after your surgery, show them how the player works.)

– **Post-op** (where you can do the most good)

Homeopathic Arnica orally

Arnica gel (not on fresh wound)

Reiki, which is hands-on healing

Chiropractic (great for pre-op also)

Massage (great for pre-op also)

BF&C (Dr. Christopher has a formula; check online)

Don't forget your ice

Stretch as recommended

Visualize faster healing, the wound knitting together, the tissue growing back

Reframe pain as sensations of healing

Listen to your customized hypnosis tapes or see your hypnotherapist for pain management and healing

Do scar tissue massage on the wound when appropriate

AAAAAAAAH! STRESS

How I came to be interested in mind/body is an interesting journey all its own. I've been involved in massage for over twenty years and, although we think of massage as a purely physical modality, we can't escape recognizing the role of the mind and the spirit in the healing process. The more bodies I put my hands on, the more I saw the connection between what people were saying and thinking, and what was being acted out in their physiology. Carolyn Myss, a five-time *New York Times* bestselling author and internationally renowned speaker in the fields of human consciousness, spirituality and mysticism, health, energy medicine, and the science of medical intuition, describes this phenomenon when she said, "Our biography becomes our biology." And I have definitely seen this to be true.

What I was observing in my practice piqued my interest to go further than just massage and I started investigating. I debated about chiropractic or physical therapy school. But nothing was ringing true to me. I heard the word naturopath and after seeing the definition, knew it was my path. But even after I achieved that goal, I wanted more. After I finished my ND as a traditional naturopath, I pursued a Masters and PhD in Natural Health. Through all those classes and degrees, I began to learn more and more about the mind/body connection. Add to that numerous classes at Harvard Medical School on the topic and my own reading for fun (Yeah, I read medical books for fun; doesn't everyone?), I began to learn some theories and develop some of my own about health that proved true almost every time I used them in my practice.

First off, there is no separating the mind and the body. We cannot think and believe things without them affecting us in some significant way. If we tell ourselves enough times that we are worthless or stupid or sick or unhappy, we will start to physically exhibit symptoms of such. In the same way, by incorporating positive self-talk, visualizations and affirmations, we can cause positive changes in our bodies and our lives. I also strongly believe that stress is by far the biggest disease we are facing. (I know I just told you a few paragraphs ago that stress isn't the problem, but for the rest of this section I'm going to use the word stress as opposed to stress response. You'll know what I mean.) And I'm not alone in this belief. Early in human history, the stress response, which we'll get into in detail later, was a necessary function for our survival. In modern society it is not quite as useful as it used to be and is oftentimes, in fact, detrimental to our health. Dr. Herbert Benson coined the phrase Relaxation Response in opposition to the stress response. I will teach you ways to utilize the Relaxation Response, not only for your health, but for that of your friends and family as well.

I have also found that not only does negative language and thought affect us, but often our stress gathers in certain vulnerable parts of the body, which seem to have phrases that correspond. For example, if we feel like our hands are full, we might manifest hand pain or carpal tunnel syndrome. This was one of the first client examples that made me aware of this mind/body connection. Author Louise Hay has similar theories about dis-ease (out of ease) and how its location in different parts of the body corresponds to stresses. I talk about this in depth in my chapter on Somatization and will give you ways to uncover these verbal hints for more complete healing.

What follows are some of the warning signs of stress. See how many apply to you.

<u>Physical symptoms:</u>

Headaches
Indigestion
Stomachaches
Sweaty palms
Sleep difficulty
Dizziness
Back pain

Tight neck and shoulders
Racing Heart
Tiredness
Ringing in the ears.
Restlessness

Behavioral symptoms

Excess smoking
Bossiness
Compulsive gum chewing
Critical attitude of others
Grinding of the teeth
Overuse of alcohol
Compulsive eating
Inability to get things done

Emotional symptoms

Crying
Nervousness/anxiety
Boredom, nothing has meaning
Overwhelming sense of pressure
Anger
Loneliness
Unhappiness for no reason
Easily upset
Edginess, ready to explode
Feeling powerless to change things

Cognitive symptoms

Trouble thinking clearly
Forgetfulness
Lack of creativity
Inability to make decisions
Thoughts of running away
Constant worry
Loss of sense of humor

I was doing a radio show where I discussed some of the above signs and the radio host went completely silent. I thought I had been disconnected. He finally started talking again and sadly said, "Oh…I think I'm stressed. I have all of those. I had no idea." Ooops.

So, first off, what is stress? One of my favorite definitions is "a threat, real or imagined." Often it's something coming from the external world that we think we don't have the resources to deal with. It has a lot to do with feelings of *powerlessness, hopelessness and helplessness*. It has been observed throughout time that those three conditions lead to increased disease. From a physiological perspective, it's a cascade of catecholamine hormones, such as adrenaline or noradrenalin, which facilitate immediate physical reactions associated with a preparation for violent muscular action. These include the following: [2]

-Acceleration of heart and lung action

-Paling or flushing, or alternating between both

-Inhibition of stomach and upper-intestinal action to the point where digestion slows down or stops

-General effect on the sphincters of the body

-Constriction of blood vessels in many parts of the body

-Liberation of nutrients (particularly fat and glucose) for muscular action

-Dilation of blood vessels for muscles

-Inhibition of the lacrimal gland (responsible for tear production) and salivation

-Dilation of pupils (mydriasis)

-Relaxation of bladder

-Inhibition of erection

-Auditory exclusion (loss of hearing)

-Tunnel vision (loss of peripheral vision)

-Disinhibition of spinal reflexes

-Shaking

---

[2] Henry Gleitman, Alan J. Fridlund and Daniel Reisberg (2004). Psychology (6 ed.). W. W. Norton & Company. ISBN 0-393-97767-6.

The fight or flight response was very important to our development and helped us survive to this point. But now, that innate response isn't as useful and is in fact, somewhat detrimental to our health. We are no longer being chased by a bear, now we are being hounded by the subtleties of the kids on drugs, the IRS, the angry boss, the sick cat and the mother in law with Alzheimer's. It's not dynamic and shortlived. We have no time to recover. This harms almost every aspect of our health.

In the stress response, the immune system is at first heightened to help us fight any infection. But if we continue to operate in this heightened state of stress for prolonged periods of time, the immune system starts to weaken and disease can take hold of us. Historically, after the danger passed, hormone levels would decrease and we would sleep. Now with our stress at a constant level, we don't get that break. This explains the all too common situation of a person who works under constant pressure to meet a deadline, and when she finally allows herself to go on vacation, she gets sick on the first day. Her body finally has a chance to rest and the virus can take hold.

A body under stress often has trouble with proper digestion, sleep, sexual function and nutrient absorption. This is why being in a constant agitated state is not only bad for our health but also leads to more prescriptions and medical interventions.

As I mentioned, the opposite of this stress reaction is the Relaxation Response (coined by Dr. Herbert Benson), which calms the stress response and releases feel-good hormones. Whereas the stress response is very helpful in warning us against immediate danger and getting us moving to react, our current stressors are not as dynamic. It's not a saber tooth tiger around the corner that eventually moves away so we can recover; it's the economy, the IRS, our spouse, job insecurities, our kids, our boss, and other daily stresses that don't seem to subside. These constant, low-grade stressors don't allow our body the natural downturn in the hormones, followed by sleep. When we don't get a break from our reaction to stress, it starts to manifest as problems in our bodies. Studies have shown that increasing the Relaxation Response not only slows heart and respiratory rate and decreases blood pressure, but it also slows the genetic expression of aging. That's right: relax more, age more slowly. Stress also affects our sleep cycle and brain function. This is why numerous experts from every facet of medicine estimate that 60-80% of our doctor's visits are due to stress-related disease. Some report as high at 90%. The same statistics are applied to workplace accidents.

Another aspect of stress is that our body can't distinguish between what we are imagining and what is happening external to ourselves. This is why we can have dreams during sleep that are so real that we wake up scared or mad or guilty that we slept with the paperboy. So in the same vein, by using our thoughts and fantasizing about something that's not really happening, we can cause a change in our physiology and stress levels. We are actually forming new connections in the brain constantly (called plasticity) and thinking something over and over can change the neural pathways. This is why imagining negative situations or worrying about things that aren't real can make our bodies react so negatively, and why creative visualization and affirmations work.

We have all had experiences where we get ourselves so worked up over something that we made ourselves sick. This is why it is extremely important to only think positive, productive thoughts. We get enough stress from the outside; we don't need to be making up any more inside our heads.

Now that we've talked about stress, let's see how dealing with this stress response can help you. I read a recent study where it was discovered that rats having an outlet for their stress did not develop stress-related disease. Distraction is another great stress reliever. Some of the most basic human hobbies act as a distraction. These distractions and outlets also remind us of what is truly important. This is one of the most common and efficacious ways for humans to reduce stress.

The more control we feel we have over our stress is important. If I tell you something stressful is about to happen, you have time to prepare and plan. You can utilize your coping strategies. It's also great if you know how long it will last so you can look forward to the end of the stressor. If it happens when you don't expect it, it tends to have more of an impact. Where that effect is reversed is if you have too much notice and can spend time ruminating and worrying about the future. Often when we experience stress we have to displace it somewhere. This can frequently come out onto another human, typically an innocent bystander. We can't control the stress at work or the traffic, so we yell at our kids when we get home. Social support during stressful times is incredibly important and helps us displace the stress. The key is remembering that stress isn't the problem and that we have options to control our reactions. Stress is partially feeling helpless and hopeless, so taking any portion of control will help. For more detailed info about stress, see my multi-award-winning book, *Conquer your Stress with Mind/Body Techniques.*

Man in an Elevator

When I was living in Los Angeles, I stopped at my doctor's office after hours to pick up some prescription samples that were left for me. I walked over to the door, found the bag, got my inhalers and headed back to the elevator. When I got there, I saw a very agitated young man. He was swearing under his breath and looked completely out of sorts. I asked if he was okay. He explained his wife just had a baby and there was a mess-up with the insurance. They were not covering certain things and he came down to deal with it. But nobody was listening and no one was around and he was very upset. He went on and on as we waited for the elevator.

When we stepped into the elevator I said, "You just had a baby." He said, "Yes." I asked a little boy or girl? He said it was a little girl. I said, "And everyone is healthy?" He nodded. "I know you're upset about the insurance thing, but the bigger picture is that you have a beautiful baby girl at home and your wife is healthy. Why don't you go spend the weekend loving them and experiencing this new fabulous thing? None of this other stuff matters; it can wait until next week." He just looked at me, his eyes got very wide and he said, "You know what? You're right." It was evident to me that in that moment we were brought together for a specific purpose. I totally understood he was upset but the larger thing was he was blessed with this miracle. His focus was on the wrong thing.

I have thought many times about that man in the elevator and what he must have been going through. I totally appreciate his frustration. But it's important to remember there are things bigger than ourselves that must come first and *we* control where we put our focus.

MEDITATION: CAN'T YOU JUST SIT STILL AND BE QUIET?

⸻

Let me preface this chapter by explaining that I am very Type A, an only child, incredibly competitive, triple Capricorn, control freak, daughter of a dad who wanted a son. I constantly heard as a child, "Can't you just sit there?" Or, "Why don't we see who can be quiet the longest?" And my favorite, "Sit down, you're making me nervous." I do hip-hop and flying trapeze for fun and stress relief and I've been a dancer my entire life. Sitting still is not my strong suit; turning off my mind is not something I'm good at. So the times that meditation was introduced to me, I not so much fought it as I just failed at it. I acknowledge now that there is no such thing as failure. I can simply say it wasn't my strong suit. I would sit and I would try, and my mind would wander, and my to-do list would start or something would itch and I know I wasn't supposed to scratch it or my foot would go numb or my hand would tingle. I found it to be quite a miserable experience.

A yoga teacher attempted to teach me breathing; it was the most frustrating thing ever. Apparently I don't breathe properly either. I can blame that on dance, where you were to hold your stomach in very tight, and I found myself breathing into my chest. When the yoga instructor tried to get me to belly breathe, I just couldn't do it properly. It made me feel sick and lightheaded. So, with a combination of all of those things, meditation has never been my strong suit. I can sit on the beach and stare for a long, long time but my mind is wandering, taking a journey elsewhere. So when I started doing my dissertation for my PhD and meditation was one of the things I was writing about, I pondered whether it was something I could do now at this point in my life. I tried it and ... still not very good at it.

I found myself a few months after my dissertation sitting at Harvard Medical School at the Benson Henry Institute for Mind-Body Medicine, studying with multitudes of physicians. When the instructor announced to the class that we were going to meditate, I thought, "Oh, crap." She asked how many of us had a meditation practice and I turned behind me to look (I sat in the front row, of course I did) and many hands went up. She asked how many people thought they couldn't meditate and stared directly at me. For a long time. I slowly raised my hand and she nodded knowingly. Did I have a giant Type A embroidered on my shirt? She was going to go over the rules of meditation. I turned to a clean sheet of paper, ready to write down the multitude of things you had to do. You had to sit a certain way, with your hands in a certain position, with your tongue on the roof of your mouth somewhere, with your eyes rolled back in your head and if you itched you couldn't scratch and then you floated away and turned into one million bubbles. Or so I thought. Her rules were: 1. Concentrate on something repetitive. 2. When thoughts intrude, dismiss them without judgment.

What?! That was all there was to it? There were only two steps? That I could do. Let's try. She had us close our eyes and concentrate on our breath. The rise and fall of our chest or the feeling of the air going in and out of our nostrils. Don't switch back and forth, just pick one. On our inhale we were to think, "I am...," and to do that with every inhale. On the exhale we were to think, "...at peace" and do that with every exhale. We did that repeatedly for about five minutes. She reminded us that if other thoughts intruded, we should dismiss them without judgment, just let them float away like clouds on a summer day. She finally went to count us out of the meditation and she asked us to open our eyes, to which my response was to shake my head no. I didn't want to come back. I opened my eyes and she was staring at me with a big smile and gave me a little knowing nod. I had mastered it. Okay, I didn't exactly master it, but I could do it. We did many meditations several more times during the week. And I found that with every time, I got more and more involved, more and more relaxed. It was bliss. These have since saved my life. Or at least the lives of those around me as I'm screaming in traffic or getting irritated that the airplane is late again. I have taught these meditations to millions of people. Between radio and TV interviews, magazine articles, and in my own books, I have certainly spread the word about the power of the mini meditation. I have to say the joy of the mini meditations is that you can do them anywhere. Standing in line at the bank, waiting in line at the post office, sitting in traffic, before you speak, write, perform, take a test. This calms the stress response and puts us into what Herbert Benson called the Relaxation Response. Try it. It will change your life.

A great illustration of what the mini meditation can do was one of my experiments with BioDots. BioDots are sensitive measures of temperature that you put on the space between your thumb and your pointer finger on your non-dominant hand. We came back from lunch one day at Harvard to find these sitting at our place at the tables. We each put one on and the instructor explained that if they stayed black, we were stressed or cold, and if they changed color from yellow to green to blue to a bright purple, we were relaxed. She expressed that it was not a competition and we should pay no attention to what was happening with anybody else's dot and also that it was not broken. That every single class someone came up to her at lunch and told her that their dot was broken. "The dot was not broken, you were just stressed," she said. It was very cold in this conference hall so for most of the day a lot of us stayed with black dots. What was funny was at lunch we were all standing out in the sun with our arms up in the air trying to get our dots to change color. Mine never did. I became bummed and was sure she gave me the broken one.

After the seminar that day I had found myself a hip-hop dance class. I rushed from the conference hall to the hotel to change, jumped in a taxi and went over to Cambridge. It was a little nerve-racking. I didn't know what kind of dance it actually was, would I like the music, would the other kids like me? I became a thirteen-year-old all over again. My dot was still on and I noticed that about halfway through dance class, it turned blue. I got very excited until I realized it went promptly to black (it also could only get so warm and it was quite hot in the classroom).

After dance class I left the studio and jumped into a taxi. I looked down at my hand and saw that my dot was bright purple. It was also the time when I felt that post-exercise euphoria overtake me. That feeling of getting out of the cold pool and putting on a warm sweatshirt. I got back to the hotel very excited about my dot. It was bright purple by then and I felt fabulous. I took a shower, with my hand outside the curtain so as not to disturb my dot, got out of the shower, got dressed and settled into the hotel restaurant with a glass of wine and a nice dinner. Looking around, I could see dozens of people staring at their hands and slightly smiling. Clearly they had been in class with me and had found a state of relaxation and a purple dot.

After a while I realized I should call my husband, as he was on the West Coast and I was about to go to bed. He asked me how my day was and I proudly told him my dot was purple. "Oh, um, okay." Obviously he didn't know what that meant but figured it was important. We talked briefly for just a few moments and then he asked me about the cat. He said the cat wasn't feeling well and didn't look right and he wasn't eating his food. Please understand, this cat is his life. The cat has his own book, movie, calendar, Facebook posts and now phone case cover. I told him if he was concerned about the cat, he should take him to the vet the next morning. That I was 3,000 miles away and couldn't really help. As he talked more and more about the cat, he got more and more agitated. He wasn't mad at me nor were we having a fight, he was just getting upset. As we're talking, I looked down and saw that my dot was fading. I finally said to him, "Look, honey, I have to go. You're turning my dot black." He didn't understand what that meant but did get that it was a very serious matter.

I got off the phone with him and looked at my dot. It looked pathetic and I didn't know what to do to regain it. What I decided to try was to sit on the edge of the bed and do a mini. I spent just three minutes doing the "I am at peace," opened my eyes and saw that my dot was purple once again. It was an amazing illustration of multiple things. One was simply how powerful these meditations are. The other was how powerful stress can be: even when we don't feel stressed, our bodies can actually have a physiological reaction. It was quite telling, and I shared that story the next day with the whole group.

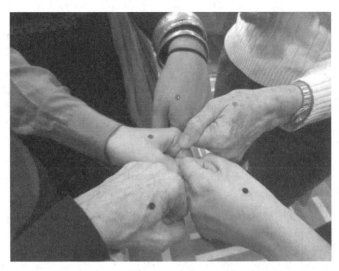

Biodots around the world

But, for those who want to go further, to really sit on the pillow and meditate, what do I have to offer? The following year I got brave. I studied meditation and visualization again at Harvard, with a gentleman named Daniel Brown. Whereas the first classes I took at Harvard spanned an entire week, this meditation and visualization class with Daniel Brown was only three days. But I learned so much. He works frequently with athletes, judges and attorneys in ways to use visualization to enhance performance. He also taught very formal seated meditation. And as reluctant as I was at first, I found myself getting into the rhythm of the breath and finding that I could not easily do it, but I could do it.

He led us through a visualization where we would find our ideal self.

Picture yourself in a room watching television and on the television is you doing something amazingly well, with ease and grace. It goes on from there. I found this to be incredibly useful and for the longest time, before dance class I would do an abbreviated version of that visualization and found the routines came so much easier for me. The visualization I had on the TV screen was me dancing with ease and grace and perfection with a smile on my face, but it would apply to anything I was about to do.

Dr. Brown teaches around the world and helps people to develop more formal meditation skills. He was amazing. A little intimidating, but amazing nonetheless. We talked about daydreaming and that scattered brain and he helped us to focus our thoughts and our attention on what we truly want to achieve. Being mindFUL instead of mindLESS. As with any class, even though I was with hundreds, there were moments where I thought he was talking directly to me. We had to sit to meditate, and I found this incredibly difficult, as we were tightly squished into a room that should've held a certain number but they had about twenty more chairs shoved in. I was touching the people around me and at first all I heard was every cough, throat clearing and rustle of paper, but soon I found myself able to relax and let myself go. The last meditation of the conference I actually did find myself turning into one million tiny bubbles and floating away. It was heaven.

If I can do it, you can do it. Seriously, you know my background. I'm not one to sit still and be quiet and definitely have trouble quieting my brain. So really, if I can make this happen in my life after a few short days, then you can too. I'm not proud to say that I haven't particularly continued my meditation practice. I bought a pillow and it's in my office staring at me collecting dust. But I continue to do my minis multiple times a day and occasionally with urging from my spirit, I sit on the pillow and try to quiet my brain and still my body. Sometimes I get it and sometimes I don't. Sometimes I leave from the pillow to return a client call, because, in quieting my brain, I remember things I was supposed to do. Or I have a brilliant idea and I have to write it down. To me that is a benefit as well. If I can clear my brain and stop the chatter enough that the important things come forward, that is a win. I encourage you to try to get on the pillow, or at the very least do your minis. They are life-changing.

GLASTONBURY QUEST

One of my dreams as a child was to visit Stonehenge. When my husband was asked to go on a press trip to Germany, and I had never yet been out of the country, I announced that I was going. He explained that because it was a press trip, I wasn't invited. "No offense." I said, "No, no, you misunderstand, I'm going to England." And I started to plan my trip. The arranged tours that were offered weren't going to get me to the locations I wanted to go to. So I decided to rent a car and do it myself. Many of my friends freaked out about that. "How can you drive on the wrong side of the road, on the wrong side of the car, in a country you've never been to?" Valid question, but I knew I'd be okay. I spent three days in London without a car before I decided to undergo my trek into the countryside.

Kathy at Stonehenge

My first stop was the phenomenal, the amazing, Stonehenge. I didn't realize you could see it from the road and as I drove by, tears came to my eyes. I felt like I was home. I parked the car, which, by the way, I actually enjoyed driving. And practically ran to the henge. I stood there for the longest time thinking about the millions of people who had crossed between its ancient stones. The laughter, the tears, the deaths, the births. I pondered, as so many had before me, who made it and why? But it was time to go. I bought a packaged sandwich and headed to my next location: Woodhenge. You didn't know there was a Woodhenge, did you? Very few people do. I did tons of research on this area before I left and knew that it was just a few miles up the road. A henge is a Neolithic earthwork; this one was a series of wood pylons made in quite an amazing pattern.

From there I was heading to Avebury and Bath for my final destination, Glastonbury. I got to see the white horse on the hill. I stood in the center of the stones in Avebury. I visited the bathhouse in Bath, wishing I could stay longer at that location. It was phenomenal. I headed to a small village called Stanton Drew where a henge was literally in someone's backyard.

And for a pound donation, I sat amongst the stones. It was pure magic. I decided to sit in the direct center and meditate – something I was not able to do at any of the other locations. As I was meditating, I heard a sound rise up from the stones around me. I wondered if it was the cows or the sheep that I had to walk around to get into the circle but I realized it sounded vaguely human. When I finished my meditation and turned around, I realized there was a group of about four women who were vocalizing, improvisation-style. I spoke to them briefly and they said they were fascinated at the meditation I was doing and hoped their vocalization helped. It certainly did.

The sun was about to set and I had about twenty-two miles to drive before I got to Glastonbury. I got in my car, turned on the radio and gleefully drove toward Glastonbury. I had about seven miles to go when a truck came around the bend into my lane. I swerved to avoid it and my tire hit the low wall that was on the side of the road. The tire blew. I was furious. I found myself stranded seven miles away from my goal, by myself on the side of the road. Luckily, I opted for a global cell phone and I called England's version of AAA. They were going to send someone.

I then called the bed-and-breakfast where I was to stay to let the owner know I was going to be very late. I was furious. I was so close to my goal. Why me? Why is this happening? It's my dream vacation. And it's ruined. I just wanted to complain to her. I wanted to bitch and whine about how horrible the situation was. But that wasn't allowed to happen. When I, in a panic, explained my situation, she was very calm. She said, "Are you safe?" That took me aback; I didn't expect her to ask that. "Yes, I am safe." I started to complain about how this was so unfair and she interrupted me by saying, "Are you looking at something pretty?" *What?* "Are you looking at something pretty," she asked again. I stumbled on my words and said, "I...I don't know." She said, "So you sit. You wait. You look at something pretty. You'll get here when you get here." I was outraged, with her and her attitude of being all so healing and grounded. I wanted to call an American friend and complain about how horrible the situation was. But instead I did just as she instructed. I sat and I waited. When I turned behind me, I realized I was looking at the most amazing vista, as the sun was setting on these golden hills. There were trees and sheep and cows. It was truly one of the most beautiful things I've ever seen. I sat on that wall and stared for about thirty-five minutes before the British AAA truck came, changed my tire and I drove on to Glastonbury.

This lesson for me was huge. Sometimes it is about the journey, not the destination. I was only an hour behind schedule. It was not a catastrophe. She was right, I was safe. And I took the opportunity to look at something pretty. And her words have echoed through my brain in countless situations. Her wisdom and the wisdom of Glastonbury has stayed with me forever.

The Tor in Glastonbury

VISUALIZATION: DAYDREAM YOUR WAY TO HEALTH

Visualization has been a part of my life since high school. Again I learned this from someone "very accidentally." We'll talk later about the concept of accidents and whether everything happens for a reason or not, but for right now, let's just say I very accidentally learned visualization. I was in the summer stock production of *Oklahoma*, it was my big community theatre debut and about four days before we were supposed to open, I started to not feel so well. I sat at rehearsal with a giant cup of hot tea with lemon and honey and one of the other cast members asked if I was okay. "I don't feel well, I have a sore throat and I'm starting to lose my voice," I told him. I got very upset, as I had to sing and dance and this was my big debut and I couldn't possibly miss opening night. "Have you ever visualized?" he asked me. I looked at him like he was crazy. I mean, I was only fifteen years old. What the hell did I know about visualization? "Do you daydream?" he then asked. I said I did that all the time and I was also an only child so I could talk to myself too if I needed to. He said that was perfect.

He asked if I could visualize my immune system. Again, I must've looked at him like he was nuts. What the hell does the immune system look like? He explained that I should picture a place behind my heart. I know that now to be the thymus gland. He said that was the center of the immune system and that I should picture white light or coolness coming out of that area and rushing into my throat. He explained that we actually have the ability to activate the immune system. He asked if I had ever seen those movies where at the end the cavalry comes rushing over the hill to save the day. I told him I had. He said that's what it's like. The immune system starts and white blood cells rush into the area flooding it and overcoming the bacteria, virus, pain or whatever it was.

I did as he instructed. I lay in my bed that night and I visualized my immune system. I pictured white light and heat rushing in from the area around my heart and completely covering my throat. I had a clear visualization of these white blood cells cascading into my throat and filling the entire area with light and heat. Then the cavalry came. There were cannons and horses and a huge battle ensued. I must've fallen asleep sometime during the Great War because when I woke up the next morning, I didn't have a sore throat, I never did get sick, and I was brilliant as chorus girl number three in *Oklahoma*.

It's fascinating because I never once listened to him explain this to me and thought, "Wow, what a whack job. Why in the world would I visualize my immune system? He's an idiot. He's weird." Those thoughts never crossed my mind. I believed that I could make any reality I wanted. I have a vast imagination and a huge ability to be creative.

I've been visualizing since then. When I was in college I auditioned to be a dancer on a cruise ship. In the midst of warming up for the audition, I was doing high kicks above my head, my stable leg came out from underneath me and I fell flat on my butt on the hard concrete floor. I got up, shook it off and went ahead with a three-hour dance audition. After the audition I was exhausted and went straight to bed. Worst idea ever. I woke up the next morning and could barely move. The pain and inflammation increased over the ensuing weeks until I could no longer sit comfortably in a chair for more than about ten minutes. So if you were a freshman in college at Point Park in Pittsburgh in the late eighties and you saw a woman lying on a heating pad in the back of the room, that was me. Not the easiest way to make friends as a freshman in college.

Tylenol and other pain meds were doing very little and I finally went to the orthopedic surgeon who was recommended by my college. I sat there with my father as the doctor showed me on the X-ray that I had a cracked vertebra. He told me it looked like a pretty bad crack and I would probably need to be put in a back brace for six months. Oh, hell, no. I was not about to contain myself in a large plastic back brace. I was dancing, I was acting, I was modeling. A brace was certainly going to interfere with my life. The doctor said they could do it over the winter so I would have a sweater on and no one would notice. What an idiot.

They were going to confirm how deep the crack was with a full bone scan, 360°. Then I would be fitted for the back brace. The scan was scheduled for two weeks later. I got back to my dorm that night and pondered what I could do. I remembered my *Oklahoma* friend telling me about visualization and I thought maybe that would help. But visualizing the immune system wouldn't do anything. What could I do, what could I do?

I suddenly had a very clear image pop into my head, a construction worker. He looked like a Super Mario Bros. guy and he had on a little hard hat, denim shorts and work boots, a tool belt and carried a toolbox. I realized I could send him to my back and he could fix the problem. So that night I lay in bed and I pictured this construction worker walking up to my spine, checking it out, investigating it, looking it over and then he pulled out a little caulking gun. And he squirted caulking into the place that was cracked. Then he took his little trowel and smoothed it out. I did this every night for two weeks straight. Sometimes he had caulking or cement; sometimes he had a plate with rivets, which he drilled into place. I noticed as I continue this visualization every night, my pain decreased. And I felt like I had better mobility.

Two weeks later I had the bone scan and I sat in the doctor's office to compare the two images. The X-ray on the left, the bone scan on the right. He counted up the vertebrae on the X-ray and then to where the crack should be in the bone scan and, much to his surprise, there was no crack. He turned it this way and that, flipped upside down, turned to face the other way, confirmed the names and he could still not discover a crack on the bone scan. He finally gave up trying, turned to me and said, "I don't know what you did. But you just saved yourself six months in a back brace and you – gesturing to my father – a lot of money."

I have used visualization for countless things since. If I do feel like I'm getting sick, which is incredibly rare, I use the immune system visualization for my throat, as that's typically where I feel it first.

I had a very bad flying trapeze accident. I came down wrong in the net and basically almost ripped my little toe off. I had a dislocation and about five stitches between my toes. I was told to stay off my foot for ten days. I gasped to the doctor and said, "I have a dance show in ten days." And he said, "No you don't." I knew that I had the ability to speed my healing so I could do that dance show in ten days. I get into more detail in the chapter on healing and surgery (pg. 115), but let's just say the construction worker (and his crew) really did their job.

When I was writing my dissertation for my PhD. I had a section on visualization. Little did I know that there were dozens of studies backing up what that cast member told me so many years ago. Studies have been shown proving visualization can help with sports performance, immune function, blood pressure reduction, even changing the temperature of our limbs. We have such a vast ability we don't even begin to utilize. Our brain is amazing, but it doesn't understand the difference between what we are thinking about and imagining and what is really happening. That's why, when we have negative scenarios running again and again through our thoughts or we dwell on something negative from the past, we're actually sparking the stress response in us.

Animals don't do that. They don't come back from the hunt and make excuses as to why they didn't catch that buffalo. They don't dwell on it for days. They don't worry about their performance the next time. They need the buffalo so they just go out and do it. That's how they survive. So those brilliant imaginations that have given us computers, movies, books, literature, all the inventions we have today, are also from those enormously creative brains that can make our lives hell with our imagination.

There are so many uses for visualization other than wound healing and boosting your immune system. We can visualize outcomes; we can visualize ourselves in situations in which we want to see ourselves.

I truly believe that so many of the things I have accomplished come from the fact that I imagined them first. The stronger you can feel it, the stronger you can see it, the stronger the outcome will be. At the very least, it stops our stress response and puts us in a better place to deal with the things that we are given. And the important thing to remember about visualization is that you can customize it to whatever works for you. Not everyone has a construction worker. Maybe it's an angel swooping in and taking away pain or inflammation. Ants carrying away the tumor, soldiers, army men, ice melting. Make it whatever works for you.

I had a cancer client who was suffering greatly. Much pain. She had esophageal cancer that had grown so much you that could see the tumor coming out of her neck. She was terminal. Nothing but a miracle was going to save her and she was coming to me to relax and decrease pain. I would do Reiki on her and rub her feet. I would lead her through a visualization during her sessions where angels would swoop in and carry pieces of her tumor away. She was obsessed with angels; her house was filled with them and she herself was an angel. She would picture it, she would smile lightly, eyes tightly closed, sometimes she would cry. Did it make her tumor go away? No. But she said it decreased her pain. It made her feel like she had one thing that she could control in a situation where she was totally out of control. It made her feel like she could make a decision about her own care in a world where people were just doing stuff *to* her. And she said the time with me, with the visualizing, was the only time she didn't have pain.

Explore what visualization can do for you.

I Write this Chapter
Effortlessly: Affirmations

In learning to change our minds, I've found that one of the simplest and most effective techniques is using affirmations. Some experts estimate that we have around 60,000 thoughts a day and that 50,000 of those are negative. That's 80% negative thoughts, which translates to me as 80% negative results. It's so easy, especially with what's happening in the world today, to let our thoughts go to fear, worry and fatalism. And it is important to acknowledge our feelings and note that we do have fear and concern, but when these thoughts start to rule our minds and become repetitive and distorted, as we talked about in the previous chapters, it can lead to illness and negative changes in our bodies.

Add to this that 60-80% of visits to the doctor are caused by stress. If we look at our lives at this exact second, where is the stress? Seriously, look at this moment in time. What is wrong? Our thoughts, and thus our stress, are often in the future and usually about something that we're not even sure is going to happen. We talk about it, think about it and dwell on it, even if it's not guaranteed. Like we learned before, we can't control our emotions, but we can control our thoughts. I'll teach you another way to do that. We've talked about emotion/body correspondence, mini meditations and the stress response. The next technique is affirmations, using positive language to program our lives.

I find this especially useful when negative thoughts interfere with my ability to fall asleep. Try repeating the following phrases, "I fall asleep quickly and easily. I wake up feeling refreshed." These types of short phrases do one of two things. Either they program me to fall asleep quickly and wake up feeling refreshed or, at the very least, they shut out the other thoughts that are running through my head. There is a physics axiom that states, "Two solid objects cannot occupy the same space at the same time." The same principle applies with our thoughts. We can't be thinking two things at once. That's what counting sheep is all about; it distracts us from those repetitive thoughts that plague us at bedtime. I'm not saying changing our thoughts and words is easy. On the contrary, it can be quite hard at first. Especially if we have been programmed to think negatively since we were young or are surrounded by negativity in our lives. But it can be done with a little practice and the results are phenomenal.

When working with affirmations there are a few rules of thumb.

Make them short.
Keep them in the present tense.
Make them positive.
And repeat often!

So don't say "I'm not sick anymore." Rephrase your wording to "I am healthy and well." Saying "I want to be rich" puts the emphasis on the future and focuses on a current state of lack. Saying "I am wealthy and abundant" or "Money flows easily to me from unexpected sources" creates a positive present-time scenario.

So you can see that affirmations can do more than just attract good health. Here are some more examples.

I am wealthy and prosperous.
I am healthy and well.
My body is strong and resilient.
The universe provides for me.
I am divinely protected.
I attract love and support.
Supportive, helpful friends surround me.

I could go on and on. The most important thing is to recognize situations where you tend toward negativity and decide to change your mind. Going into situations with a negative attitude doesn't benefit anyone and just makes life more unpleasant.

It's easy to incorporate affirmations into your life. Take some time to work these into your day by saying them at a certain set time or keeping them posted on your mirror, car dashboard or desktop. This is especially important if you are prone to negative thinking about your body or certain situations. Changing the speech from, "My neck always hurts" to "My neck is strong and healthy" can start to induce physiological changes. Once affirmations become part of your life, you'll be more in tune with when your thinking and words have become negative. If you'd like help, have a friend or loved one *gently* remind you when you get off track.

Similar to affirmations is setting intentions. My Reiki Master, Diane Vaughn, always set intentions before the Reiki attunements that she provided. I didn't really understand it back then, but now I am a believer in their importance. Often, when we set an intention for something, it becomes easier to achieve. She used to phrase them this way:

My intention is to co-create with the universe true healing for my body, mind and spirit. (Or whatever it is you are trying to achieve.)

She always started intentions, no matter what they were, with "co-create with the universe." Then she wrote them down for me and asked me to repeat them throughout my day.

It only takes a few moments to do the intention process. Take note what areas you would like to change and create (co-create) and design phrases that are empowering rather than limiting. The more we can expand our beliefs and consciousness, the more our worlds will expand with them.

For those of you interested in the studies that I found on affirmations, visualization and our language, check out my book *Conquer your Stress with Mind/Body Techniques,* where I list many studies.

IT'S ALL ABOUT
ME: ADVOCACY

I see clients on a weekly basis who complain about their healthcare. Either the doctor is running way behind, gives them poor information, wrong information or they feel unheard. Sometimes it's out of the doctor's control and sometimes I see people who are getting shoddy care. I see this especially with the elderly population. I had a client who would get a urinary tract infection almost every six weeks. I asked her why she wasn't seeing a urologist and she remarked that her primary care doctor told her she didn't need one. That he would not tell her anything different. So, she didn't go. Instead she took highly concentrated antibiotics multiple times a year. She had no clue of the cause of the infections and her doctor seemed to care less. To me, that is shoddy medicine.

I have seen countless examples of things overlooked throughout my career. A client came to me recently to see if I could help her migraines. I asked her if they were actually migraines or just really bad headaches. All she knew was she was given three different medications. And they didn't seem to be helping. We spoke for about fifteen minutes before her massage and I asked her what she did for a living. She was a receptionist. I asked her what side her headaches were on, she said the left. I asked her if she held the phone at her work between her ear and shoulder, she answered affirmatively, on the left side. I figured out her headaches. About ten minutes in to the massage, her whole body relaxed and she said her head no longer hurt. Her headache was gone. We talked about stretches to do, about getting a headset, about staying hydrated and I sent her on her way headache-free.

I have the privilege of time when I see my clients. Doctors don't get as much time as I do. I've uncovered numerous underlying problems that doctors didn't find. I'm lucky that even though I'm not a medical doctor and I don't diagnose or prescribe, I'm a keen observer and I take the time to really think about what might be causing my client's issues. And I refer them accordingly.

We have to be our own advocates. No one knows our bodies like we do or cares as much as we do. Sure, our spouses, kids and friends care, but they are not inside of us. Do refer to these people to help us notice changes in our bodies or behavior, but we need to pay closer attention to us. Take a few minutes each day to check in to how you feel and what your body feels and looks like. If you don't know what you feel like when you are well, how can you expect to be able to describe what is going on when someone asks? Here are some more tips about advocacy.

~Ask questions.

Medical professionals have a habit of tossing a bunch of Latin at you, hoping parts of it are understood. I've also observed them telling things to partially unconscious patients in a hospital bed. During meetings, many patients nod their head and then later realize they have no clue what was just told to them. If a doctor or nurse tells you something that you don't understand, ask them to clarify, take notes or bring someone with you.

Questions like, "How long will this last?" "Are there any side effects with that drug?" "What will that test show?" and "Can you explain what those results mean?" are great questions to keep in your mind.

And make sure you get copies of your blood work and test results and file them. It's your right to see these results and it can clear up questions later if you develop a condition and need to check for patterns, or switch medical professionals. I believe you can't have too much information about your condition, medication or projected outcome.

Some people get very nervous or embarrassed when they see their doctor; this is understandable especially if you have a serious condition. Prepare your questions in advance, in writing, when you are calm and have time to think. Talk to others who may have had what you do or have some medical knowledge. Often they will know things that you would never think to ask. Capitalize on their expertise and input. I have clients ask me all the time about communication with their health professionals.

~ Do your own research.

So, you've gotten a Latin name or set of initials for your condition (IBS, PMS, RLS, ALS, PTSD, it goes on ad infinitum…that's Latin). Well, what the heck does it mean? It's very important to know everything about what you've just been told. Doctors often have handouts or will give you as much time as you need to have it explained to you. A lot are on a limited time constraint, though (under seven minutes), so you might walk out of the office with a few initials and a prescription. This is where YOUR research comes in. With the advent of the Internet we can find information about anything. Now, that's both good and bad. I've had clients thoroughly convinced that they were dying because they saw something on the Internet. And others who research their condition so completely they could get a degree in it.

Common ailments are easy to locate online and many have support groups or bulletin boards where you can post questions and comments. Be careful where you get your information, though. Don't believe every post on every bulletin board and don't rely too heavily on blogs and notes from laypeople. Web MD is great and any site affiliated with a university or hospital tends to be pretty accurate. Though they typically don't recommend alternative and complementary therapies. Double check your information by using multiple sites.

Now, what if you prefer to take a more alternative approach to your disease, dysfunction or disorder? There are great resources for that as well. Again, check to see who is sponsoring them and don't rely on just ONE for your information. Be aware if their website is mainly a sales pitch for a product or gadget; of course they're going to say it works. Doublecheck your sources.

~Seek out more.

Don't be afraid to get a second, third, or fourth opinion if something doesn't sound right to you. Not every medical professional knows everything. Commonly, things are misdiagnosed or over-/under-diagnosed. You might have to convince your insurance, but do it if you feel that it's needed. Also explore alternative practitioners. I've helped clients fix problems that were muscular that were totally overlooked by their medical team. They apparently forget we have soft tissue. We have to have a team. A team made up of different players. We can't have all quarterbacks or goalies.

~Know thyself

As I mentioned before, it's so important for us to be in touch with our bodies and to know if something feels right or not, and if something is working. Trust yourself; you are living inside your body and know it better than anyone else. Track how medication makes you feel also. I had a client taking a pretty heavy-duty seizure medication for her headaches. She came to my office with symptoms that I suspected were side effects from this drug. The more she took the drug, the worse these conditions got. Her doctor wanted to give her MORE drugs for these new conditions (called iatrogenic disease – caused by medical treatment). I finally asked her if the headache medicine was even working and she confessed that after six months her headaches hadn't changed at all. She was afraid to tell her doctor, but I encouraged her to. He pulled her off the meds and, though her headaches were still there, all the other problems disappeared. Sometimes you have to be your own detective. Owning a *PDR, Prescription Drug Reference*, is a big help. You can also find common side effects on line. And sometimes the side effects can be worse than the initial condition.

I have another client, a young lady who was experiencing shortness of breath and chest pain. When she went to the doctor and explained that, he simply said, "Well you know you're fat." She explained that she did indeed know she was fat but she's been fat all her life and never had this problem. He recommended she lose weight. The problem persisted. She went to Dr. number two, explained her issue and he said that she should probably lose some weight because she was simply obese. She said, "I've been fat all my life I've never had this problem before." With doctor number three she heard the exact same thing, that she was simply overweight and that was the cause of her problem. She demanded a chest x-ray. What the chest x-ray showed was she had blood clots growing in her lungs. She could've died. Had she not demanded that test would probably not be with us today. It was very easy for the doctors to simply dismiss your problem as being overweight but she knew herself and demanded good care.

~Get help

Let's say you've been admitted to the hospital, your family is far away and you're too sick to do your own research. Try to have someone as an advocate for you. This can be as simple as friends who can double-check things or a paid caregiver. It's particularly important to have someone there when a doctor is explaining things to you, especially if you're sick, weak, exhausted or unconscious. It's also useful to have someone present to make sure you're eating, wearing your hearing aid or glasses, double-check what meds you are getting, get you to the bathroom and the like. If you have no one to help, there are volunteer advocates and people who are paid for this service (some hospitals can provide them). Search online for one near you or ask at the facility where you are staying.

A client was recently in the hospital and, without anyone asking if it was needed, a stool softener was prescribed. He had had his gall bladder out previously and was already prone to loose stool. This poor patient found himself trying to rush to the bathroom and releasing his bowels all over himself, the bed, the floor and his booties. The nurse was informed to take the stool softener off the chart. Later that day, another stool softener arrived with the pills. Luckily we caught it before it was given. Two more stool softeners arrived over the next two days because no one ever took it off the chart. These things happen and it can be a lot more serious than just poo!

It's a shame that we have gotten to this place, where we have to be so on top of our medical care. But for now, that's the way it is. Take control, ask questions and be your own best advocate!

A side note: There are fabulous physicians, hospitals and nurses. I'm definitely not implying that everyone is incompetent, but in the case of your health, I'd rather be safe than sorry.

SUNRISE, SUNSET

My boyfriend and I spent a weekend in Solvang, CA. At the end of that weekend we were going to go to his house in Glendale. I was ecstatic to get there. For some reason we had to drive separately, so I raced off in my car, he in his. At that time I had a choice of either charging my phone or putting in my radar detector. I chose radar detector so I could speed as much as I wanted to get to his house and enjoy the rest of the evening. I got to his house in Glendale in record time and I waited and I waited and I waited and I waited. Finally, about forty minutes later, he arrived. His face was slightly fallen, his countenance was slightly sad. He asked where I had been. I told him that I couldn't wait to spend the evening with him so I raced home. He said, "I know, I was trying to call you on your phone. The sunset was so beautiful I wanted to stop and watch it go down over the ocean with you. But you were so far ahead of me and your phone was off." So he pulled over and watched the beautiful sunset himself. I did not have the ability to be in that moment with him. I was projecting into the future and I missed a phenomenal opportunity to spend time with him. This is a lesson that has also stayed with me for a long time. And I'm sad I missed that moment with him. Now married, we have certainly had many other sunsets. But this one stands out as an opportunity missed.

Kathy and husband, Michael enjoying the sunset

MINDFULNESS: IN THE HERE AND NOW

T here is a general misconception about mindfulness. People often use the word mindfulness as interchangeable with meditation and they picture people sitting around on pillows *om*-ing quietly to themselves and clearing their minds. In reality, mindfulness is just *being in the present moment with curiosity and focus.*

We can do any task mindfully. You have to do the dishes anyway. So do them with full presence and concentration. Notice how the water really feels on your hands. Is it warm enough, too hot, too cold? Watch the bubbles form as the soap mixes with the water. Feel the texture on the plates; is all the food coming off? What about the lemony smell of the soap? As you watch the bubbles form, perhaps one floats away and you watch it rise into the sky. A little rainbow exists within and at some point it pops with a little spray of water. Use all of your senses to fully engage in that task. Soon you find yourself with a kitchen full of clean dishes and you have just done a mindfulness exercise.

You can do this with any task. It's great because many of these are things we have to do anyway. For example, taking a shower, brushing your teeth, cleaning your house, driving to work, making love with your partner. When was the last time you were truly one hundred percent present with all of your senses during lovemaking?

I had the privilege of studying with Thich Nhat Hanh at Harvard. He and about sixty of his brothers and sisters instructed us on mindfulness. After the most amazing exchange with the monk talking to us about mindful eating, we did a mindful meal, where about 1800 of us ate in silence. I don't know if you ever heard 1800 people eating in silence, but I can assure you it is nothing but silent. You could hear the chewing, the packages and the occasional spffft as a soda opened up and everyone would look. Soda is not mindful. I ate my sandwich and my yogurt over the course of about half an hour. I truly tasted it. And I can tell you it didn't taste very good. I wouldn't have noticed it otherwise, as I normally just shove my food into my mouth to get to the next activity. It was completely eye-opening, and every-other-sense opening to see what our food truly tasted like, smelled like and what it felt like in our mouths.

Before we started our portion of the meal, the monk onstage held up a piece of broccoli. He stared at it for the longest time. And you could feel 1800 pairs of eyes on him, leaning in closer to see what he was going to do. He stared at the broccoli for what seemed to be forever and finally smiled and spoke. He said, "This broccoli is a miracle. Someone put a small seed in the ground. And at some point someone else watered it and the sun came down from the sky to warm it. Soon a small sprout rose out of the earth and started to grow. More people tended to it, watering and nourishing it. The rain came and the sun beat down on the small plant until a little flower formed. Eventually it grew and grew, greener and greener, until broccoli became apparent on that stalk. Then someone picked the broccoli, cared for the broccoli, packaged the broccoli and brought it to you. This broccoli is a true miracle." We were all practically in tears. It was the most eloquent, beautiful thing I've ever heard, and about broccoli, no less.

After we had our meal, not as articulately as the monk, we then did a walking meditation where the thousands of us descended on the streets of Boston. It was amazing. We walked in silence through the streets and by the time I got to the park to do the seated meditation, I looked behind me and there were still others pouring out of the hotel. We stopped traffic for blocks. At first people honked, impatient to get to their location (which I totally get), and then they became curious. They started stepping out of their cars and taking pictures of the monks and us as we slowly walked on the street. We then sat in the park and did a fifteen-minute seated meditation that was led by Thich Nhat Hanh. It was phenomenal.

I felt like I wanted to communicate to the monks about how moved I was by this experience. Because we were in silence, we were told to write down any questions or comments we had. I rummaged through my purse in an effort to find something to write on. I had nothing. I finally located a pen and a small piece of cardboard. I wrote, "This has been the most amazing experience. Thank you all for coming and sharing this with me." I went to hand it to the monk closest to me and it was the hot one. Yes, there were two very hot monks.

First I felt guilty about thinking he was hot but the woman next to me agreed, he was pretty hot. I handed him the note and he bowed to me and smiled. He took it and read it, bowed again and walked off. It was then I realized what I had written on: the card the hotel gave me with my room number on it. Leave it to me to pick up the monk. He never did show up to my room. Thank God, as I don't think I could've passed that off as a religious experience to my husband.

Descending on the streets of Boston

Since I returned from my journey, I have assigned a certain number of tasks a week to do mindfully. For people who don't think they can meditate or don't have time to meditate or don't understand the concept of mindfulness, start out slowly. Take five minutes a day to enjoy a mindful meal, walk, cleaning session. The benefits are staggering.

MOVE TO SB: TAKE TWO

⌗

T here was one point in my life in Los Angeles that I was the associate producer of a documentary film company. I loved the job but my frustration was that, in order to have it, I wasn't allowed to audition anymore. I essentially gave up my dream as a performer. Sure, I would do some shows in the evenings, but daytime was relegated simply to work. I was starting to feel a pull northward. I didn't want to be in LA any longer, especially if I couldn't be auditioning for things. My bosses were out of town, my then boyfriend was out of town, and I set out that day to find myself a job in Santa Barbara. I flipped through phone books and did what little Internet research I could with the Internet still in its infancy. I faxed resumes up to production companies, heard back from a couple saying they wouldn't hire me unless I lived there.

But one called me back immediately and said how ironic that I had responded to his ad so quickly. I questioned what ad he was talking about and told him I didn't see an ad, I just happened to be submitting a resume that day. We made arrangements to meet that weekend to talk about his production job. I became very excited about the prospect of getting to move up to Santa Barbara. I interviewed that Saturday morning and he hired me on the spot, even offering me more money than I asked for. We talked about partnerships and eventually me taking over the company. I was very excited and thought this was the opportunity I was waiting for.

I started to make arrangements, quit my job in LA, found an apartment in Santa Barbara and about two weeks later found myself living in a town that I always dreamt of living in. I had found an old journal where in 1988 I said my dream was to live in Santa Barbara. And that dream had become reality.

The man who hired me was, let's just say, difficult to work with. He was incredibly high-strung, very successful but a little neurotic and demanding. He would change things on a moment-to-moment basis and I had trouble keeping track of exactly what he wanted from me. It was driving me crazy. I was miserable and found myself getting sick. I finally decided I could take it no more and quit on the exact date he claimed he was going to fire me. What I found out later from other staff is that his full intention was to fire me all along. All the talk of partnerships and me taking over the company was just a ploy to get my LA connections to do one shoot and then I would be gone.

Suddenly, as quickly as I had found myself living the dream, I was humiliated, scared, unemployed and not sure where to turn. My life was wrapped up in either performing or production. Both of those avenues ended in Santa Barbara. I floundered, floating, trying to decide what to do. As you can imagine I'm not the best at floating. I either want to swim or get out of the pool. But this was a pivotal moment for me, as I pondered what I wanted to do with the rest of my life. I took a day job working for an eco-resort company. Within a few weeks of my taking the job, which I have to admit was pretty interesting, they announced that their funding had ended and they would be shutting down.

At that time I realize I was aching more and more to get my hands on people and do massage. My then boyfriend, now husband, and I would walk down State Street and I would look at people and say, "Their shoulder is high; they must be in pain. Their low back is out; they had knee surgery." It was driving my boyfriend crazy and he finally said, "Look, clearly you have a passion for this, just go do it." So I did. I investigated the few massage schools in town and finally decided which one I wanted to attend. Though I had had years of massage experience on paper, I didn't have the needed hours to get licensed in Santa Barbara.

I signed up for school and the day I did, my company announced its closing date. The closing date was ironically the first day my massage school started. The next day I looked in our newspaper and found a job listing for massage therapist in a physical therapy office. I applied and was hired on the spot. I explained that I wasn't licensed in Santa Barbara yet. The director said that was totally okay because it was a physical therapy office and I would be working under the supervision of a physician. I took the job. The thing that worked out so perfectly was that I needed hands-on hours for school. Whereas most people were begging family and friends to get free massages, I was working forty hours a week – about thirty of which were me actually putting my hands on people. I tore through my hours in no time and as soon as I graduated I became licensed. I lasted for just a few months more at the physical therapy office; their ethics and insurance fraud really got to me.

I started my own practice and here I am today, sixteen years later. For the longest time I was angry at that man who brought me up to Santa Barbara for the production job. But I began to see the plan that has unfolded. I had to go to Santa Barbara but never would have done so without a job. Had the production job worked out, I never would've left, as it was perfect. I needed to get to Santa Barbara and then be promptly turned loose. The man who I thought was an evil insane dictator actually was one of the greatest gifts of my life. And in looking back through other similar situations where I thought there was a failure, I realize it was the most amount of growth and opportunity I'd ever experienced. The lesson with this is that we just never know what the situation is going to lead to. There is no good or bad; there just is. We as humans have to label it as positive or negative. But ultimately we don't know the answer.

There is a great parable I like to quote. A farmer came into some money and was able to buy some extra horses. The villagers surrounded him and said, "You're so lucky you get all these extra horses." He said, "We'll see." The next day his only son went out to train the horses to plow the field and he fell off and broke his arm. The villagers once again gathered around and said, "Oh your only son has a broken arm. What horrible luck." The farmer said, "We'll see." The following week the army came through and took all the young boys to be soldiers. The son could not be taken because he had a broken arm. The villagers once again gathered around and said, "It's so lucky your son broke his arm." The farmer simply remarked, "We'll see."

We just never know what the outcome of our experiences is going to be. Try to take each and every one as a neutral experience, learn what you can from it and know that what sometimes seems to be the darkest time can lead to the greatest light.

CHAKRAS, CRYSTALS AND GEMSTONES: ROCK ON!

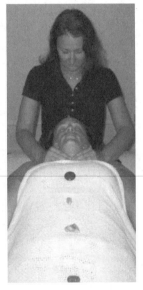

Reiki with gemstones

As a child I was fascinated by rocks, gemstones and crystals. Every year when we went on vacation in Virginia Beach, one of the souvenir shops had a giant bin of stones from which you could pick. I always wanted some. I actually toyed with the idea for about ten minutes of going into geology just because I thought stones were fascinating. I still remember the three types of rocks: Igneous, Sedimentary and

Conglomerate. (Once I said Ignatius, sedentary and conglomerate. Not quite right.) And that's about all I remember. I had a book on healing and spirituality when I was a child and it talked about the chakras and how to use stones and gemstones on them. It also talked about color healing and how different colors corresponded to the chakras. I had an old crystal that had belonged to my grandmother and I used it as a pendulum and on my own chakras. I had no idea what I was doing but it seemed to be something that I was interested in.

When I was studying with my Reiki Master, the chakras were very important in what she was doing for healing. She would put her hands on the different chakras and just feel if they were open or closed, or she would use a pendulum. Then she would pull gemstones out of a beautiful bin and place them on the chakras in order to open them up. I was taught that chakras are to spin clockwise (other opinions differ), meaning that you are taking in just as much energy as you are giving out. If they are stagnant, closed, blocked, or spinning the wrong way, they need to have healing. Some people can see the chakras, those swirling vortexes of color. Others can feel them. Others don't believe they exist, which is totally okay too.

The way I use the chakras now is the same way I was taught. I use crystal or gemstone placement after I check in with the pendulum during a Reiki session. I have also had some massage clients ask specifically if I could do a chakra balancing on them. It's merely a balancing of the energy in the body, similar to what acupuncture would do. It's that chi, that universal life force in those seven points, and there are believed to be hundreds more points. You can feel the energy gathering.

Here is some more technical information about chakras and their correspondences.

First: Root Chakra, base of the spine, red, physical security

Second: Sacral Chakra, midway between navel and base of the spine, orange, body and issues around body

Third: Solar Plexus Chakra, behind the navel, yellow, control, power

Fourth: Heart Chakra, over the heart, green, relationships, forgiveness, love

Fifth: Throat Chakra, at throat, blue, communication, speaking your truth, asking to have needs met

Six: Third Eye Chakra, center of forehead, indigo, the future, spirit, beliefs

Seventh: Crown Chakra, top center of head, violet or white, God, spirituality, divine guidance

For crystals and gemstones, there are hundreds of books written on what each crystal does, what it means, what its properties are. Some of the more common crystals you'll see people using are amethyst, rose quartz, citrine, smoky quartz, lapis and hematite.

I have a very large and beautiful tray of varying sizes of crystals of various colors, shapes and purposes in my office. Usually they are used specifically for my Reiki healing and I don't often go by what the books say, I go by what jumps out at me when I am thinking about what the client needs. I usually go by the color correspondences: red, orange, yellow, green, blue, indigo, violet or clear. And I grab the color stone that stands out and I place it on the chakra. But I don't always do it that way. For example, I have a string of rose quartz chips that sometimes I place over the entire torso of the client. Sometimes I will have them hold a larger crystal or a rose quartz if they feel like they need to attract love into their life.

Every time I travel and see a store that sells stones, I get very excited. Recently I was doing a meditation and talking to my higher self and my guides. It was expressed to me that when I meditate I should hold a

.certain crystal, and that I knew which one. And I did; it was a hand-sized, perfect-for-holding piece of quartz. It sat on my desk for the longest time. It was the only one that wasn't living in the tray with the rest and so now I hold it any time I meditate or need clarity. It's a perfect focal point.

I was recently at a class at my hypnotherapy school and they ended the day with a woman speaking about being a channel. (A *channel* is someone who speaks to beings or spirits who may or may not have lived before. A *medium* speaks to the dead.) I noticed that she was holding crystals in her hand as she was working and I thought, "Interesting. During one of my meditations, I was just told to hold certain crystals," as I just mentioned. I spoke with her afterwards and she shared with me that what she was holding were Lemurian crystals. I had never heard of these before. But sure enough, the following week when I was back down for another class, I popped into the crystal store next door and there was a whole bowl labeled Lemurian crystals. It was kismet. I held one, felt a little woozy and thought, "I must have one of these." I bought a whole bunch of them. And I now have what they call a Lemurian lantern in my office on a lighted rotating stand. It is beautiful and shoots the most amazing colors around the room. It definitely has some sort of special energy. Do I believe that it actually was held in the hands of someone from Lemuria, an advanced ancient civilization, as rumored? I don't know if I can go that far. But it is beautiful and definitely brings peace to my office.

Science would say that though rocks, crystals and gemstones are pretty, they don't have any healing or magical properties. Those who use them for those purposes will disagree. And again, my philosophy is this: it's not harmful, there are no side effects, you don't need a prescription. If wearing or holding or meditating upon a stone or crystal makes you feel good, then do it.

One way you can work with crystals is to use them directly on your body. As I mentioned, I put them on the chakras to help balance them during a Reiki session. You could also find one that vibrates for what you're looking for and wear it as a ring, necklace or carry it with you in a pocket or pouch. You can use gemstones and crystals to charge water. Put them in a glass of water and charge them with either the sun or the moon. Reportedly, those properties will then go into the water. If you are using crystals in your life, make sure you cleanse them often by running them under water, or setting them on another large crystal and charging them under the full moon.

Oftentimes things we are attracted to are things we need in our lives. If you find yourself really drawn to a certain stone, go ahead and wear it; it's probably doing you some good. If you think this is a bunch of bunk, that's okay too; just ignore this chapter. As I've said before, not everything works for every person.

HYPNOSIS: YOU ARE GETTING HEALTHY

⟨———⟩

Hypnosis as a formal modality is pretty new to me. Self-hypnosis and past life regression were always things I was interested in. In fact, I did my first past life regression in high school. Recently I studied hypnotherapy at the Hypnosis Motivation Institute in Los Angeles (www.hypnosis.edu). I found the program to be fabulous. And a great addition to the modalities that I already do. Being that I deal with a lot of clients in pain, dealing with stress or looking for self-improvement, this was perfect.

My first exposure to hypnosis was when my mom was sick. She had gone to see a pain management specialist who gave her a hypnosis tape. One side of the tape was the ocean and the other side guided her through meditation for pain. I remember her listening to it maybe once or twice and then it got handed down to me. I loved listening to the ocean side, though I do remember on occasion listening to the self-hypnosis side on the reverse.

When I was in college, I found myself fascinated with past life regression. If this is something you don't believe, then I totally respect that. Frankly, it doesn't matter if it exists or not; it is a phenomenal therapeutic device. Anyway, I found myself incredibly interested in it. I studied with Roger Woolger, who was doing a seminar in Pittsburgh. I excitedly attended. I was definitely the youngest person there and probably the only one who was not a psychotherapist or psychiatrist. I sat mesmerized (no pun intended) as he hypnotized the entire audience. He then brought up one woman and did specific therapy on her. She looked like a different person when he was done with her.

I decided this would be fun to play with. So I found myself on Friday nights regressing my friends. Everyone else was at frat parties, ordering pizza and drinking too much, and I was playing with past life regression hypnotherapy. I was a different kind of kid.

I didn't really do much else with hypnosis until I got to California. I did a few past life regression classes and read some more but didn't pursue it very much. When I moved to Santa Barbara, I met Peter Wright, with whom I started doing some regressions. I found that the more lives I explored, the more healing I found within myself. These sessions explained habits, mindsets and relationships with other people. I do believe we travel with the same folks over and over. I think we've all had the experience where we meet someone for the first time and feel a kinship, a feeling that we've known them forever. It's like a coming back together. And in the same way, we barely see someone and we know we can't stand them. Could this be related to a past life? Could that explain chronic pain, stuck cycles, prodigies and soul mates? I think it could. And the more I explored past lives, the more real it seemed. But frankly, even if they were stories I made up wholly out of my imagination, they propelled me forward.

What I learned about hypnosis from HMI was vast and fits so well in with my philosophy of healing.

I learned about the knowns and unknowns in our unconscious mind, how those things formed in childhood still influence our attitudes, decisions and feelings today. Through dreams, imagery and hypnosis, we can pass the critical mind and make real change in our unconscious beliefs. We know we want to quit smoking consciously, but something deep inside ourselves keeps lighting up. Hypnosis is great for helping to change behavior and allowing people to live to their full potential.

I also learned that much of the population walks around in a suggestible state of hypnosis. About forty percent of the people who come into my office have to be *un*-hypnotized before I can hypnotize them. No wonder we are so susceptible to negative comments, inferences and "feelings" we get from others. We're hypnotized. That feeling on the freeway where you're not sure if you passed your exit, or you 'come to' and don't know how you got home? That's hypnosis. A hypnotic state is often caused by an overload of stimuli, like stress, high emotional states or a feeling of being overwhelmed. Or something lulling us into a state, like staring at a movie, or watching your professor drone on and on. Sometimes I find myself drifting away and I'll actually count myself out of hypnosis. 1,2,3,4,5, eyes open. Wide awake. And I feel how different my body and mind feel. Try this yourself, especially if you are getting drowsy on the road.

I also learned about working with what is called the Mental Bank (https://hypnosis.edu/streaming/mental-bank/), which is a tool to change our internal script. What I mean by that is, we all form certain beliefs about our lives that come from observations and situations from our childhood. If we see our parent struggle and struggle and fail at every job, there is a certain script that forms in us that maybe we have to fail at everything too. We have all known someone who, it seems, at every turn has 'bad luck.' Nothing ever goes right for them, seemingly by no fault of their own. And we know others where everything they touch turns to gold and even though they may be jerks, untalented or irresponsible, they succeed. Often it's our inner dialogue that propels these events forward. We can change that script and Mental Bank is a great tool for it.

Working with a qualified hypnotherapist has boundless applications and benefits. Try it for yourself and see what tapping into your unconscious can do.

How My Injuries and Surgeries Help Others

This is actually an interesting situation in that usually when something bad happens to us or we are in pain, we simply complain about it. And I have absolutely had those moments. But what I have learned is, when I'm in pain or I need to have surgery or I'm having an ailment, usually soon after, someone else has that exact same issue and I can help them through it. For example, my thyroid. I have talked to countless people about my experience with thyroid surgery and having to take thyroid hormone.

I had a very young client having abdominal pain. She went through very invasive gynecological exams, X-rays, MRI, and no one could find anything wrong. I finally asked her mom if it was on the same side as her previously treated low back pain. It was. I had her come in. I did a psoas release, something I've dealt with personally in the past, and all her pain stopped. I think it's important to rule out scary medical issues, but also important to remember soft tissue and muscle involvement. (The psoas is the muscle that runs from the low back through to the front of the body.)

I learned so much about my body from having my own ribs "go out", throwing out my back, having knee and toe surgery and experiencing things that needed my chiropractor or acupuncturist or surgeon. I can now practically tell you over the phone if you have a rib out and need to see a chiropractor because I know exactly what that feels like. (Not diagnosing, just sharing info.) All of these things I learned because of my experiences with the pain. I think so much of what has happened to me has simply been so that I can experience it and help others through it when they have that same issue. It might sound bizarre but at least it's giving me a way to look at my ailments and issues in a positive light.

EMPATHY, OR DO YOU FEEL WHAT I FEEL?

S ince I was a child I have felt things deeply. Perhaps many of you reading this can relate to that. I got upset in crowds, feeling overwhelmed with the energy. I had trouble going to nursing homes or funerals because I could deeply feel the grief and sadness, even if I didn't know anyone in the home or those who had died.

Empathy is defined as a deep emotional understanding of another's feelings or problems, while sympathy is more general and can apply to small annoyances or setbacks.[3] But this type of empathy goes deeper. It's not just walking in their shoes, it's feeling their blisters. People who can actually feel others' feelings or pain and help dispel it are referred to as *empaths*. I don't think it's possible to talk about the mind/body connection and my journey without acknowledging that others' emotions and pain can have a profound effect on us.

When I first started my practice, I would take on the physical pain of my clients. I didn't know how to stop it, but I would be left feeling exhausted and sick after almost every session. I could also feel people's pain in crowds and groups of people, which was just annoying. Once I started doing Reiki, I noticed that the phenomenon was greatly lessened and though I would still feel and sometimes express people's repressed emotions, I didn't take on the physical pain. Here are a few examples from my own life.

---

[3] Retrieved from http://www.thefreedictionary.com/empathy November 20, 2011

A close friend of mine at the time was in a play and as I sat in the audience waiting for it to begin, I began to get anxious and nervous. My anxiety progressed to the point where I thought I was going to vomit. I knew it wasn't mine. I got up, went back stage, found him looking sick and pale and told him to stop it, that he was making me sick as well. He confessed that he was having pretty bad stage fright all of a sudden and did some breathing exercises to calm down. As he calmed, I calmed.

My husband was doing a relay race called the Hood to Coast in Oregon. One of his co-workers was running it also and we were all shoved in a van to head to the next exchange spot. I was between the two men. About a mile from the site, I started to feel really anxious and began to get incredibly nervous. I looked over at my husband and he was calm and laid back. I was confused. Where was that coming from? I realized I was touching the legs of both runners. I turned to our friend at my right and asked him if he was nervous. He answered in the affirmative, telling me he always got nervous right before a race. As soon as he got out of the van and started running, I felt fine. Now, I don't necessarily understand the point of me feeling someone else's sadness or nervousness or anxiety, but I wonder if it would be worse for them if I didn't dispel some of it.

Here is another example of empathy from my own practice. I was doing Reiki on a woman and she clearly had energetic issues with her throat. She couldn't wear tight necklines, turtlenecks or short necklaces. I was doing Reiki over that area and she started to get emotional. I was suddenly and unexpectedly overwhelmed with the desire to cry. Just as I started to feel that, she said, "I'm not going to cry, I'm not going to cry. I don't want to cry." So, I did. It seemed that I was channeling her feelings because they were too much for her to handle.

Often, though, people who are empathic find the feelings heightened with certain populations like children or animals. I feel very sensitive around animals. I had a theatre director whose cat was pregnant. And this cat was *very* pregnant, belly almost dragging on the ground. We were sitting around reading a new script and the cat meandered into the room and sat right on my lap on the floor. Within a few moments, I had incredible cramps that actually doubled me over. I started making horrible noises from the pain. Everyone stopped and looked at me and a few seconds later kittens started to appear. The cat went into labor and I felt every contraction. As soon as the cat was taken off my lap, all the pain went away.

Empaths have a deep sense of knowing. They can suffer others' pain, feel their emotions and are highly sensitive. Many people discover this skill as children and find themselves confused and overwhelmed at what they are experiencing. Some children are ostracized by their peers or told to just "suck it up" and "not let things bother you" by unknowing parents and teachers. These children tend to be more sensitive to things like crowds and emotional movies. *Bambi* might not be the best choice, as the child will empathize so strongly when Bambi's mother is killed that he/she might be upset for days as I was.

Though a lot of people believe this is a skill that you are born with, some believe that it can be learned or at least honed as you get older. Most people discover it accidentally and assume everyone is like them. The surprise comes when you share an experience and people look at you like you're crazy. Many empaths choose bodywork and healing as their profession. And I have definitely found that my massage and healing ability has benefited from the intuition and empathy that I use during my sessions. I get a lot of compliments on my massage. With some clients my expertise is from years of having my hands on people, technique and reading lots of books, and sometimes my hands are just guided and they say, "How did you know that was the spot?" Sometimes that's what it is, just a knowing.

For people who come to us as clients, this skill can be deemed everything from weird to unbelievable to extremely impressive. Most of the practitioners I spoke with never shared what was happening with their clients. They feel that this is just part of their job and that it's not appropriate to burden the client. If you are an empath, I encourage you to examine your motivations if you are going to start telling people about it. Some people feel this skill makes them a superior healer and they start to get wrapped up in the ego boost that comes from showing off. New healers and egotistic practitioners can use this skill to manipulate clients. I caution this behavior as it borders on codependency and can lead to negative results for both you and your clients. If you are going to share, take a moment to ask yourself why.

Now, you fit the description of an empath, you have the gift. What the heck do you do about it? Learning to feel without taking on too much is a skill that takes some practice. We certainly don't want to suffer or have to leave society because we're so overloaded. I consulted numerous practitioners and other resources to find what the best way was to control this energy; here are some of the answers I found:

~Meditate, specifically on the throat and root chakras.

~Be choosy; stay away from "psychic vampires" who want to zap your energy.

~Learn to put up an "energetic shield."

~Donna Eden in her Energy Medicine healing videos suggests zipping up your energy like a coat and locking it by placing your tongue behind your top teeth.

~If you feel you're taking on others' emotions, repeating your own name over and over can be helpful.

~Watch your diet, as foods high in sugar and alcohol can deplete you. Protein, especially meat, tends to be more grounding than vegetarian food.

~Engage in a spiritual discipline.

~Practice self-care, whether it's massage, retreats or a hot bath. The more depleted you are, the more vulnerable you are to others' energies.

~Some people rely on crystals for protection, like boji stones or quartz crystals.

~Others can just "shake off the pain" by shaking their hands in the air.

~Learn to be the bad guy; it's not your cosmic responsibility to fix others.

~Find a teacher, mentor or guide. Often people appear when the time is right.

~Spend time in nature. Let the trees or the earth take the excess.

~Respect yourself. If you need a break, take it. Take the time YOU need to recharge.

~Learn energy work. After I learned Reiki, I was less apt to take a client's physical pain, but still able to instinctively find it on their body. It acted as sort of an energetic GPS for me.

~Take a break from too much negativity. Avoid the news, the newspaper and the needy neighbors for a while so you can recharge.

~Try to remain positive and realize that, as hard as it is sometimes, this truly is a gift that can benefit others.

As you grow and mature as a healer/empath and acquire a stronger sense of self, you will find that the empathy grows and changes as well. I no longer take on clients' physical pain, I am often just guided to the cause. And I let the emotions wash over me and hopefully, when that happens, they get a healing benefit from it.

I encourage you all, healer and non-healer, empath and non-empath, to explore the above techniques. The only things that can come of self-exploration and evolution are positive.

PARALYZED

I received a phone call to work on a new client. She had been in an accident and was paralyzed. I didn't know exactly what that meant, as people tend to define things in different ways. I talked briefly to the woman who called me and then agreed to see her family member. I arrived to find the client lying prone in bed, feeding tube in her abdomen, unable to move, with the exception of one arm that could fly about; she could not talk, could not eat, could not drink. She basically just lay there and stared. I had never worked with someone in such a condition and I began to doubt my own ability to handle it.

The caregiver helped me remove the woman's clothes and I worked on her arms and legs and a little bit on her neck. It was very difficult to do, as she couldn't really control her movements and she was in a large bed that I had trouble working around. She also couldn't communicate with me and basically just stared at me the entire time. I wondered if she actually wanted me there. I finished the massage the best I could and they said they were pleased and invited me back. I went home that day thinking about this woman who could no longer function on her own in that body. Was that living or just surviving? Could I do that?

I thought about my life and the things I value – eating good food, drinking good wine, enjoying my husband, trapeze, dance, walking, talking and communicating my message to people. I don't think I would want to live in a body that couldn't do most if not

187

all of those things. I began to question my own mortality and if I would want to live in such a condition. I told my husband if I ever got that way to just shoot me. I wouldn't want to live. But is that true? I had an elderly client who was dying and she got to a point where I thought, "I wouldn't want to live like that." But it was those final days where she was surrounded by friends and family, got to hear everyone's praise and love for her. That was the gift of those last few days. Had she ended it earlier, she would have missed all of that. And we would have too.

We don't know what anybody's journey is on this planet. Perhaps for the betterment of my paralyzed client's spirit, this was part of her path, I don't know. Just like I couldn't understand why kids took complicated math classes in school, I can't say that this woman was not in this condition for a purpose, hers or God's, whatever your belief system is. The more I got to know her, and I didn't see her very long, I grew to understand that she *was* still there and thinking and living. I saw her laugh once and that got me so excited. I saw her watching her grandchildren grow up and her kids get awards. I began to wonder what I would truly do in that situation. But one thing it did make me do was value what my body can do in its present state. There were so many dance classes where I thought of this woman and so many like her who lost functioning from cancer, Parkinson's, Alzheimer's, ALS (Lou Gehrig's Disease), and valued what my body would do.

I find myself almost near tears with glee as I move my body in dance class and the privilege that I have in being able to dance and eat and talk and walk. Sometimes even now I grin uncontrollably at what my body is able to do. I find dance to be so exhilarating; it fills me with such exuberance that I can't imagine not being able to do it. But aren't we survivors? Do we not overcome trials and tribulations of all sizes and shapes? I have not seen this client in many, many months. Because of scheduling I wasn't able to continue her care. I wish her well and I hope she does find joy and happiness even in the condition she's in. As a tribute to her and others in her situation, every once in a while I grin when I dance, thankful for what my body can do.

MY MUSES:
DOROTHY AND ALICE

Dorothy, Kathy and Alice

I already shared with you the stories of Dr. Pat, my Reiki Master, and the gentleman who taught me about visualization. I have learned over the years that it's the people we are surrounded by who give us so much of our inspiration and information. I have had the privilege of being influenced by wise people, men and women who have entrusted me with incredible knowledge. And I've had the sense to listen (to almost all of them). Two women, though, were instrumental in my life, showing me about truly living, loving and experiencing life: Dorothy and Alice.

Dorothy and Alice, though similar in so many ways, could not have been two more diametrically opposed women. Dorothy had been married before and told me she had had several lovers. Alice was with the same spouse for over 68 years. Both had children, both bucked religion, both were politically active, both were beyond inspirational. They died at 96 and 105. Wow! Alice was more conservative, very well spoken, very educated. Dorothy, though the same level of intelligence, was a little more wild. She wore crazy hats, donned bright flashy colors. She did a striptease for her own 90th birthday. She was a crazy woman. In the best sense.

I met Dorothy after she saw my ad in the newspaper for massage. She grilled me over the phone, asking me how long and where I had studied. I was actually a little intimidated. She finally agreed that I would probably be adequate for her massage and gave me her address. She told me that she would be waiting in the back room, as she liked to take a shower before her massage. She said I should simply knock on the door, come in and say hello. I did just that on my first visit. From far away I heard a little voice say, "Come on back." I walked into the bedroom to find her standing buck naked and dripping wet. I wasn't sure what to make of that. It sort of caught me off guard. It was my first time a client had done that, and the last. She looked at me and said very proudly, "I just had a bowel movement." I didn't know what that meant. Was that a problem for her and she was so excited she had one? Does that mean she wouldn't poop on my table? The whole thing was slightly off-putting but hysterical. I loved this woman immediately.

She climbed up on the table; she would always use a little footstool that her sister had embroidered for her. I now own that stool. We would talk through the entire massage about things like religion, philosophy, sex. At one point I had walked into her house and she had an article about Planned Parenthood and sex education sitting on her desk. I glanced over it, not really paying much attention. I thought it was funny she had it there. About halfway through the massage she said, "Can I ask you a question? You seem to know a lot about a lot." I said, "Of course." She said, "Where can I find my six spot?" I said, "Do you mean G-spot?" thinking of the article I had seen on her desk. She said, "No, I'm pretty sure it's the six spot." I said, "No, I'm pretty sure it's a G-spot. Why do you ask?" "Well, I don't think I have one." I explained that she did indeed have one and using my hand as a diagram showed her where the G-spot would be. She said, "Well how do I get to it?" I said hesitantly, "Well, it's inside you. So you would need, well… a penis or a dildo." She looked befuddled for moment and then said, "Dammit, I just got rid of my dildo a couple of years ago." These were the kinds of conversations we had. As well as those about life, history, philosophy, her childhood and parents, religion, we covered it all.

I asked her once what was one of the most life-changing things that she had witnessed throughout her history. I'm thinking of things like computers, microwave ovens, Women's Lib. She was quiet for the longest time and then said, "My divorce was pretty life-changing." I told her I was thinking of more broad things like politics and social things. She said, "My divorce was pretty life-changing." I just smiled.

Very early in our relationship she was talking about her condo. It was a beautiful space. Well-decorated and fun. She told me she wanted a new couch. And new drapes. And new carpet. She had always wanted a bright red couch and was about to go get one. I was thinking to myself (out of ignorance), *You're 93 years old; what are you going to do with the new couch?* And I grew to realize it's not how old you are, it's your state of mind. When you stop living, that's when you die. That sounds silly. I mean, of course when you stop living, you die. But I mean living in the philosophical sense. Dorothy didn't ever consider the fact that she might only get to experience the couch for a day, a week, a year. In reality, she was able to have it for many years. She lived her life to the fullest every day. I want to be in my 90s wondering where my G-spot is and how to get to it. She would exercise every day on her porch. Nude. She had a fence and kept saying that no one could see her. Except for the fact that the building around her was two stories so anyone could look down on her and see her moving her naked 90-something-year-old body in the yard.

Once someone knocked on the door about the time I was supposed to arrive. She dashed (as much as she could) to the front door, flung it open thinking it was me.…it was a sales person. She was naked. We had a good laugh about that one. We laughed a lot. And if nothing was funny, she would make herself laugh every day. Either she watched or listened to something funny. Or she would just open her mouth, throw her head back and laugh until she was truly laughing. I think that was one of the reasons she lived so long. She was able to find the laughter, the humor and the irony in life. She surrounded herself with beautiful friends and family.

The somewhat unfortunate thing is how she passed. She had a stroke and ended up lying on her bathroom floor for about sixteen hours before someone found her. She had one of those medic alert buttons. But she hated wearing it so she would keep it hanging on the wall across the room. Not helpful when you fall down and can't move. She was in the hospital for a long time and then ended up in a beautiful care facility. I would drive about ninety minutes round-trip to continue her massage and her care. I did a lot of Reiki on her and a lot of talking. Near the end she was pretty much unconscious, but I know her friends and family who visited, the letters that her daughter read to her, really changed how her last few days were. I think I saw her within the week of her death. I held her hand and told her I loved her. I thanked her for the incredible influence she had on my life. She inspired me to truly live and truly experience the good things in life, no matter what your age. I think of her often and know that when I'm 93 I'm going to be just like her.

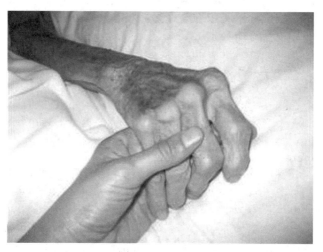

Kathy holding Dorothy's hand

Alice, as I said before, was more reserved. Wore suits of solid colors with good tailoring. She was incredibly well-spoken and very well-educated. At one point she considered being a doctor but didn't pursue that option. She and I would talk about politics, religion, philosophy. It was an incredible relationship. I met her through her husband. He was in one of the art classes I had modeled for, and asked me if I could help his wife. I saw her a few days later and then every week for almost ten years.

She said I was one of the reasons she lived so long. As much as I'd like to take credit for that, I know I can't.

She and I talked about The Great Depression and how her father was one of the few people she knew who had a job. One day a week he would dress as if he were going to work but wouldn't work that day. He would allow someone else to take his job for that afternoon so that that person could feed his family too. I'd like to think I'm wrong, but I suspect we wouldn't see that today. We talked about politics and how we had to have changes in Washington. When I asked her what her most pivotal moment in history was, she said, "I remember when I was allowed to wear pants for the first time." So much of this kind of history is lost as our elders die and our youth seem annoyed with talking to them. She and I would converse the entire hour of the massage. She talked about her exercise, her diet. She complained about putting on extra pounds around her middle as she got older. She also had a series of exercises she did every day. And she knew so much about birds. I'd describe something I saw and she could tell me what it was and what its song sounded like. Even now I see a bird I can't identify and think of Alice.

I remember showing up one day and she was sitting at her iPad on a Skype session with first-graders from somewhere on the East Coast. She was active and inspirational. She traveled around the world and she and her husband frequently recalled their travels. For a while my husband was doing some cooking for them. She would give him report cards. He still has them. She was a woman who knew what she wanted and was very successful in life. Both she and her husband dabbled in stocks. A few times she actually gave me good stock tips. I loved spending time with her, looking forward every week to my opportunity to not only learn about her life and history but also to help her through her ailments, aches and pains.

Alice is sorely missed in my life. She was a high point and inspiration and I strive every day to be more like her. I know she would love flying on the trapeze with me. And she would be thrilled that I recently went to Egypt and Jordan having no concern whatsoever for my safety. She lived life to the fullest. And near the end of her life, she remarked that there were so many things she didn't get to do. I found that depressing, as I saw her do so many things. If she could live to 105 still not getting to everything, what chance do I have? But it's something to shoot for. She kept a travel diary. I'm hoping to start the same, as often the details of those trips do fall out of our memory over time.

Both Alice and Dorothy will go down in my life history as inspirations and examples of how I would like to live my life: surrounded by friends and family, constantly educating and stretching themselves emotionally, mentally, physically and spiritually. I loved these women and their families. They were part of me. And now they go forever in my heart. I look forward to meeting them again.

MOM'S DEATH

I started this book talking about my mother dying from cancer. Of course that was a huge influence on my life. Part of it has to do with the fact that I was an only child and I think that makes us grow up quicker as well. But my mother getting sick when I was so young and losing her life when I was only eighteen was of vast importance to my development. I'm not going to get too detailed about this as I could probably go on for pages and pages. But here are just a few ways this experience changed me.

It made me want to seize the day. My mother was not quite forty-six when she died and now I just turned forty-eight. I think, *My God, I'm so young, with so much future ahead. What a tragedy that she died so young. She didn't get to travel overseas. I'm sure there were things she wanted to do that she never got to.* So to me, you "go for it," as I talked about in a previous section.

This experience taught me to not live in fear, to go ahead and take risks and take chances, because you never know when your time is up. Both my father and I have been hit in crosswalks by oncoming cars. Buildings collapse all the time. There are terrorist attacks, car accidents, drunk drivers, earthquakes; anything can strike at any moment. Even cancer. We never know exactly when our time is up. I have seen a lot of naked butts in my massage career and I can tell you there's no expiration date written on any single one. Live for the day.

And as most people assume, watching her go through what she did and my dad being such an incredible caregiver partially propelled me into the career I have now. I still can't connect the dots to make an absolute connection but I see the influence. The experience of watching her suffer allowed me to expand my mind into other choices, looking for other solutions, getting second, third, fourth, fifth opinions, whatever I need to get all the information that will help. It also taught me to listen to my instincts. On some level I think we all knew something was wrong but didn't know what to do about it.

It also taught me to have patience with my clients who are suffering. Chemo doesn't put you in the best mood and hip surgery or MS keeps you from walking your fastest. Often, I didn't have much patience with my mom. I was annoyed that she was slow, short-tempered with her requests and sometimes downright mean. I've forgiven myself, though, as I did the best I could for a teenager. But now, as an adult, I can walk slower for my client with the walker and not take personally that my cancer patient just yelled at me. I have an understanding and a grace for dealing with the suffering of others. I have that because of my mom.

And last, cherish people while they're here. You never know when you might not get to say I love you – which were the last words I said to my mom before she died. Cherish the people you love.

Kathy and mom

THE FINAL CHAPTER OR, FINALLY, PYRAMIDS

When I was a kid I dreamed of seeing the pyramids in person. I was obsessed with King Tut, enamored by the museum display of artifacts when it toured through Pittsburgh. I even toyed with the idea of being an archaeologist when I grew up. I realized, though, that I didn't want to be an archeologist, I wanted to be Howard Carter. So when I wrote in my journal at age fifteen that it was a dream to see the pyramids in person, I didn't know how realistic a dream that was. Sure, probably more realistic than singing with Van Halen or dancing with Baryshnikov (yes, those made the list as well.)

Kathy with journal entry

The Middle East is dangerous, they are all terrorists, they hate Americans. This is what I'm fed from the media and friends. But when a call for speakers came through for a conference in Jordan, I submitted. I was accepted and realized I should see where Jordan actually was. "Oh……huh, that's the Middle East. Oh, I guess I'm going." My husband was less than pleased. My father was beside himself. I was talking to a client and mentioned it was a shame that I couldn't get over to Egypt since it was a dream. She asked why couldn't I? I said, "I don't know, how close is it?" She laughed and said, "It's right next door." Huh. I guess I was going to Egypt. Thanks, Linda, for helping make my dream come true.

I decided to go; how could I turn down such an amazing opportunity? I started to plan my trip as news dribbled in about kidnappings, beheadings and people being set on fire. I checked almost hourly with the State Department. Was I being stupid? What if I didn't make it home? I had horrible paranoid thoughts of my tour guides abducting me and selling me into slavery. Thoughts of never seeing my husband again and how my dad would survive having already lost his wife. Losing me would kill him. Just when I would seriously rethink the trip I'd see a client who had traveled to those areas and told me what a blast I would have. I asked a friend in the FBI if she thought it was safe and I asked her to simply say "Don't go" if she knew of some reason I shouldn't. She jealously told me to go and have a blast. She couldn't wait to see the pictures. She said, "Kathy, you will be perfectly safe. This is what the terrorists want, to make us afraid to leave our country." At the same time as I had people excited and reassuring me, I had those go to the opposite extreme. One asked if I had checked to make sure the whole conference hadn't been faked to get me there to kidnap me. Uh…what? I was flattered that she thought I was that important.

As completely irrational as that was, it affected me. I started to not be able to distinguish between my own instincts and what I was pulling in from others. It started to shake me. I came up with a plan B, which was to divert from whatever country was scariest and go to Rome. The day finally came. It was time to go. I cried. A lot. I was freaking out and didn't know why. Was it simply the scope of such a trip? Nine flights in eleven days. What if my guide didn't show? What if the person getting my visa didn't meet me at the airport? I decided I needed to stay in the present. That what would happen on this trip was the trip. It was the flat tire in Glastonbury. I had to accept what was in the present moment and go with the flow. It was hard. I had been working on responding rather than reacting and I knew this was going to be the test of my progress. I left the house armed with multiple apps on my phone that would help, anti-nausea medication, antibiotics, tape, Band-Aids, fancy special blister socks, sleeping pills, arnica, nux vomica, even a carabiner in case I needed to make a quick escape from somewhere. Yes, I really did. The further I got from Santa Barbara, the more comfortable I became. The braver I felt. The fear started to fade. And finally as I saw my first flight was actually a go, I felt like 500 pounds had been lifted from me. If nothing else, I was going to be in Frankfurt soon.

It ended up being a truly charmed trip. Nine flights in eleven days and not one delay, cancellation, lost bag, problem with visa or issue with security. I wasn't kidnapped, beheaded, harassed or abandoned. It snowed in Amman but the airport was open when I had to fly in. The road to Petra was closed for two days but reopened the day of my tour. Yes, it was weird to see people on the streets with guns, checkpoints between cities in Luxor. Embarrassingly I was most surprised at the sense of humor of the people I met. I was so concerned with not meeting anyone's eyes, not laughing out loud and not eating with my left hand that I missed the fact that these folks are human beings. They laugh, they joke, they like to have fun. They must think Americans have no sense of humor because I missed almost all of the jokes. Another shocker to me was how much attention (in a good way) I would get from being American. I had groups of children in awe of me, wanting to talk to me, take my picture. I'd find them turning away from the antiquities and trying to capture me on video. When I waved and said hello on one camera, the gal gasped with delight and she and her friends giggled uncontrollably. It was like I was a celebrity. My guide explained that a lot of these kids live in small villages and have never seen an American. I was tempted to change the rest of my plans to visit their schools and tell them about America. But that wasn't in the cards for this trip.

It was a dream come true to be in Egypt. To stand at the pyramids was a mind-blowing dream. I photocopied my journal with the "go to Egypt to see the pyramids" line on it and took a picture of myself with it in front of the pyramids. I cried a little. When I walked up to the Great Pyramid, I cried a lot. The exact same reaction as when I was at Stonehenge. I couldn't believe I actually made it. In a world of Las Vegas and Disneyland, I had to remind myself that it was real. It wasn't a ride or a display; I was actually in a tomb that was 3000 years old or a pyramid that was older. I was in awe for most of the trip.

I made it

The only snag came when I was at Petra. My driver was going to get me at 4:30 to get me to the airport on time. He said to text him if I wanted to come out earlier . At about 3:15 I threw in the towel. I was ready to go but knew I had to walk out. I texted him to get me at 4. When I got to the entrance at 4:08 he was nowhere to be seen. I had just a slight moment of panic. I texted again and waited a few minutes. I then tried to call; it wouldn't go through. I thought, Oh my God, he has my luggage, what if he doesn't come back, what if he's stranded in traffic somewhere, what am I going to do? I noticed a hotel where I could call from, but couldn't for the life of me find the entrance. I was irritated, tired and starting to panic a bit. Finally I realized there was a guard station outside the hotel. I told them I had trouble reaching my driver and could they call him for me. I gave them the number, they called and he arrived ten minutes later. There was no need to panic, no need to feel unsure. And while I waited, I sat there and looked at something pretty. I was getting good at the responding rather than reacting.

One of the biggest lessons for me on this trip was about fear. I had no idea. As I mentioned, I heard about all the terrible things that were going to happen to me if I went. It affected me. But some of the irrational fear that I heard was really eye-opening. I had three reactions from people on this trip: most told me to have fun and be safe; my adventurous friends told me I'd have a blast, that it was the best trip they had ever done or was high on their list to do. The other extreme was borderline rude, as I had one client actually say, "Don't call me for money when you get kidnapped." He said things like that every time I saw him. I finally told him to shut up, which is not normally how I speak to my clients.

My journey instilled fear in so many people. I could see my husband, my father and close friends being concerned. But people I didn't even know, or barely knew, were freaking out. I've had people tell me I was brave for being at the Magic Castle myself, for having dinner alone, for trapeze, for going to England myself. But this, this one was really brave. And with all my debate about going, I'm so glad I went. The reality is, and I'm not trying to be morbid by saying this, you can die anywhere. I've been hit by a car, my father has been hit by a car, how many people are dying from cancer and other diseases every day. There are shootings and stabbings every day. If it was my time, it would have been my time. I'm glad it wasn't. I have too much yet to do.

I hope you have enjoyed my journey of healing (and life) thus far. If my writing has inspired you just a small bit to "go for it," to step outside your comfort zone, then I met my goal. I wish you a life of prosperity, love, adventure and a smooth but interesting journey!

Santa Barbara, California
October 2017

GO FOR IT!!!!

ABOUT THE AUTHOR

Kathy Gruver, PhD is a motivational speaker, an award-winning author and hosts the national TV show based on her first book, *The Alternative Medicine Cabinet* (winner Beverly Hills Book Awards). She has earned her PhD in Natural Health and has authored seven books including, *Conquer your Stress at Work, Workplace Wellness, Body/Mind Therapies for the Bodyworker, Conquer Your Stress with Mind/Body Techniques* (Winner Indie Excellence Awards, Beverly Hills Book Awards, Global E-book Awards, Irwin Awards, Finalist for the USA Best Books Award), *Journey of Healing* (Winner USA Best Book Awards, Beverly Hills Book Awards, Pinnacle Awards, Indie Excellence Awards and the non-fiction category of the London Book Festival) and she co-wrote *Market my Practice.*

She has studied mind/body medicine at the famed Benson-Henry Institute for Mind-Body Medicine at Harvard Medical School and has been featured as an expert in numerous publications including Glamour, Fitness, Time, More, Women, Wall Street Journal, CNN, WebMD, Prevention, Huffington Post, Yahoo.com, Marie Claire, Ladies Home Journal, Dr. Oz's The Good Life, First, and Women. Dr. Gruver has appeared as a guest expert on over 250 radio and TV shows including NPR, SkyNews London, Every Way Woman, Morning Blend in Las Vegas, CBS Radio, and Lifetime Television, and has done over 150 educational lectures around the world for everyone from nurses in the Middle East to 911 dispatchers in New Orleans, corporations around the US and teachers in her own backyard. She was thrilled to appear on the TEDx stage in February. She just completed work on a project for the military to create and institute a stress reduction program and helped shut down underground sex massage parlors in her community. For fun and stress relief Dr. Gruver does flying trapeze and hip hop dance.

A past winner of NAWBO's Spirit of Entrepreneurship Awards, Kathy maintains a massage and hypnotherapy practice in Santa Barbara, Calif. She has also produced an instructional massage DVD, *Therapeutic Massage at Home; Learn to Rub People the RIGHT Way*™ and is a practitioner with over 25 years of experience. More information can be found at www.KathyGruver.com

See you on the next adventure
Photo by Michael Cervin

References

Helpful Websites:

www.thealternativemedicinecabinet.com

www.drkathygruver.blogspot.com

www.youtube.com/drkathygruver

http://losangeles.trapezeschool.com

www.dointhemost.com

www.bachflower.com

www.corporatestressprograms.com

www.bensonhenryinstitute.org

www.abmp.com

www.hypnosis.edu

www.centerforreikiresearch.org

www.normshealy.com

www.watsoncaringscience.org

www.ronabarrettfoundation.org

http://www.flying-trapeze.com/rig-locations